Stop Lying

Getting Un-Lost and Un-Stuck in Your Life

Bennett Pologe, Ph.D.

To convince someone of the truth, it is not enough to state it,
but rather one must find the path from error to truth.
– Ludwig Wittgenstein, *Philosophical Occasions*

When a scene in a play or a movie isn't working, and we all can sense
when that is, it's because someone's not telling the truth up there.
– Bruce Willis on *Inside the Actor's Studio*

CONTENTS

INTRODUCTION

This book is about lying. I am not talking about conscious lies. I am not talking about the little boy with crumbs on his face who says "I didn't eat the cookie". He knows he's lying. I am not talking about corporations sending letters that read "in order to serve you better, we are changing our policy".

I am talking about unconscious lies. They are everywhere. A study done at the University of Toronto about 12 years ago showed that people lie within 3 minutes of social interaction and don't even realize they are doing it until they see a playback of themselves later. In the past decade or so eyewitness testimony has come under great criticism as it has been realized that people are not remotely as sure of what they saw as they claim to be – as they may honestly believe themselves to be.

These unconscious lies are destructive, regardless of how innocently, well-intentioned, or casually they occur. Throughout this book I will be presenting case examples from my office and from daily life to make this point. I am a psychologist. After almost 3 decades of doing this work, I've come to see that lying may well be the single, common error at the very heart of almost everything that goes wrong in our lives. There is often more than one lie being told at a time, and there may be layers of lies within a single person (and I'll have examples of this twisty problem), but lying is the key. I really mean this. Whether the issue is anxiety, obsessive problems, depression, irrational fears, difficulty enjoying life, indecision, difficulty loving and being loved, substance abuse, domestic violence – as aggressor or victim – or the many relationship problems that bring people into therapy, lies seem to be a central cause.

And it is exposure of those lies that brings relief, as so many different psychotherapies point out, each in their own particular lingo. Sometimes you can catch them yourself, often you will find you need a guide because of the resistance that seems built into us; resistance blinds us to exactly that which we most need to see – more about that later.

Two disclaimers and then we'll start with a few vignettes to illustrate.

First, when I talk about obsessive problems, phobias, panic, substance abuse, depression, and so on, I am not talking about the severe and extreme cases for which only intense and highly focused therapies, medication, and even hospitalization may be required. I am talking about the rest of us who struggle, for whom it may sometimes feel nearly impossible but who do manage to get through the day. Second, in trying to keep the writing as clear as possible I have used the masculine case for indeterminate pronouns throughout the text. It always seems needlessly confusing to me, even if politically correct, to alternate genders when no specific person is being described – and clarity has been my primary goal in the writing. I hope my persistent use of "him", "his", and "he" will be taken in that light.

CHAPTER 1

THE PROBLEM

Claire[1] was a 15-year-old girl who suffered from blindness and a neurologic deficit that prevented her from orienting herself in space. If I put a blindfold on you and asked you to point to the door, the window, your coffee cup, you could probably do it. Claire could not. She could not keep up with her blind peers because of this problem. She had very resourceful parents, extremely supportive and loving; they found her a great deal of extra help and special services. They also told her that he loved her, that she was a great girl, and that she could do anything she wanted. She was referred to me because of her chronic agitation, frustration, anger, tears, and fragility. One of her teachers described her as "brittle, as if always about to fall apart". She had trouble concentrating, enjoyed almost nothing, complained bitterly about trivial frustrations such as the school bus being a little late. She was quickly and easily unhinged by these minor frustrations. She cried a great deal but the tone was always one of agitation, frustration, rage. She seemed to move through the world in a state of constant astonishment that things did not go better for her. She always seemed to be crying out "how can this be?!"

Can you find a lie? One day I rather innocently observed "well of course you have trouble doing what the other kids can; you have those brain problems we read about in your medical records, remember?" The response was astounding. At first she said automatically "yeah, I know, I know". Then she stopped and for the first time her face relaxed. Her eyes welled up with tears and she wept in silence for a few minutes. This

---

[1]   The names and other identifying information of the people I discuss in this book have been altered to protect confidentiality. In making these changes I have not altered the substance of their stories or simplified anything to make a point.

was not the agitated, frantic sobbing I usually saw. This was grieving. She wept for a while and articulated "oh, that's what's been hurting me; I thought something was wrong with me!" With a smile she added, "I mean besides my eyes and my brain." Over the next few months, she made new friends, took new interest in hobbies and school, and her teachers told me she was dramatically different.

What happened? Quite simply a lie was brought to the surface. Her parents told her with the best of intentions that she could do anything she wanted. Somehow, this translated in Claire's mind to a belief that if she struggled with things it must be her fault, that there must be something pathetic and disgusting about her. Somewhere just out of conscious control, the words she heard from adults were at war with her own real life experiences of failure and inadequacy; they were lies but she could not identify them as such and ignore them or take them in the spirit intended. For whatever reason, my innocent and rather clumsy observation brought the lies to the surface. She told me in subsequent weeks "I always thought there was something wrong with me, I mean besides my brain wiring. But there isn't! I just got a really bad hand dealt to me with my vision and stuff. Actually, my friend has it much worse. Her parents are idiots."

"Bully" coined this name for himself during our sessions. His long path from childhood to my office provides a good illustration of personality development and how one can become lost and stuck. He was raised by a highly anxious, "scatter-brained" (his term) mother and a violent, impatient, and unpredictable father. Early on, he was the schoolyard bully, dishing out unto others what he suffered at home. He could recall the pleasure he felt watching another person suffer the fear, confusion, and shame that he so hated feeling at home. In grade school, he managed to develop other outlets, to channel his need to control and dominate -- which compensated for his experiences at home -- into something more productive and socially acceptable. He became a star wrestler and something of a student leader. Later, he went into the business world, aggressively and successfully working his way up the ladder of power and financial reward. During those heady years he got married, had children, and even became known as a tough but forgiving department head. He skied, threw parties on his boat, played tennis with friends and colleagues, and in all respects had a full and gratifying life.

In his early thirties something began to sour. As he described it, "everything seemed to lose its flavor". No longer satisfied, he tried new hobbies, new business ventures, even dabbled in spiritualism and religion, but nothing seemed to stop his growing irritability. He was snapping at his wife, intolerant of his employees' imperfections, and impatient with his children's age appropriate needs and minor misbehaviors. One day, in the heat of an argument he slapped his wife. Vowing never to do that again, he and his wife agreed to "time outs" as soon as he felt his anger welling up. But his discomfort and irritability were so strong that he ended up taking "time out" every time they tried to talk. Eventually they were hardly speaking. One day, riding in an elevator, he became short of breath, his heart raced, palms began to sweat, and he felt an intense need to flee. He tried to forget the incident, but soon his heart would flutter and his stomach knot in anticipation every time he entered an elevator. The same thing then happened on a bus, so he started driving everywhere. After a while, his life was riddled with phobias. In his first session he announced to me "everything was fine until a few years ago; now I have this anxiety disorder" (he'd done some googling).

What happened? There were no events in his adult life to account for this change. How did Bully go from such apparent success and contentment to the symptom-ridden and unhappy man I met at the start of treatment?

You can probably see that this fellow had developed a pattern of dominating and intimidating others in order to combat the discomfort of his own early experience of being dominated and intimidated, not an uncommon pattern. For a while it worked, first as the schoolyard bully and later via less destructive pursuits. But, as often happens in a person's thirties, the defense began to fail. It no longer contained -- shielded him from -- the discomfort of his original experiences. The energetic and ambitious lifestyle that had previously protected him from those feelings wasn't helping anymore. He consequently began to regress to his former bullying ways, to earlier modes of defense. Those old habits didn't entirely relieve the pressure, so finally anxiety took over and the panic attacks started.

It may seem obvious what was going on here, as it was soon obvious to Bully. His childhood with an abusive father and absent mother led him to compensate with bullying and rage, later with overachieving and more socially acceptable bullying; he even said once "yes I know, sometimes the old insecurity leaks through and I have panic or phobic symptoms, and I know I have trouble trusting from my childhood betrayals blah blah blah". But none of that helped.

All that analysis, however accurate, brought no relief because it failed to address some key lies. As we spoke, I began to hear things that made me question his version of his history. Here is where you might need a guide if the lies have pulled your life too far off track. With some persistent questioning the truth began to emerge. All the years things were going "great", Bully was described by many people as a great guy, life of the party, but just under the surface as very difficult to know and rather prickly. He tended to dismiss those who made such observations as "fussy and picky types". People who were closer to him saw even worse. In his wife's words, he seemed "a simmering volcano." In the years leading up to the slap, she was increasingly fearful that he would become violent. Bully also told me of waking up in a cold sweat from bad dreams he could not remember. Sometimes in the mornings he suffered from dry heaves – a feeling of vomiting but nothing came out. He managed to forget most of this until our sessions; one of his lies (to himself) up to that point was that he felt great and was doing fine.

What Bully needed to remember is not the details of his childhood but rather how bad it felt. He needed to remember the experience, not the content. This is a theme I'll be talking about a great deal in this book: The difference between real insight which heals and intellectual learning which, although perhaps fun and engaging, does nothing; it's the mental equivalent of masturbation – feels good, eases a little tension, but is entirely unproductive.

One day Bully recounted a story to me that he'd told many times over the years to friends and acquaintances, at parties and in pubs. He always told it as an entertaining story, as a joke. One Saturday when he was about five years old his father took him to the office. Bully was very excited by this trip, to see where his father worked, to be out with the old man and no sister or mother along. He always vividly recalled one particular moment: His father had gone into another room and suddenly the telephone was ringing; father called out to him, repeatedly and with ever increasing anger, to "just answer the phone", "just push the button with the blinking light!" "just answer it!" Bully always remembered his view of the office at that moment.

But telling me in session that day, he suddenly sat forward and blurted out impatiently "damn, I should have answered the phone; I was so stupid". We were both silent for a moment, surprised at how hard he was being on his five-year-old self, and then he realized that of course this was an unreasonable thing to ask a five-year-old – remember Bully had children of his own. From here came the tears as he remembered how frightened and confused he felt. This opened the door to remembering how he'd spent not only his childhood but in fact his early adulthood in that state, in dread of an almost physical attack of shame and self-loathing from his father or himself. (Could this be the dry heaves? A primitive, physical, disgust with himself?) As he reviewed his life over the next few months he realized that he always walked around expecting such an attack of censure, judgment, impatience, and worse. He had somehow managed to stop inflicting these upon others in any overt way until a few years before I saw him, although his wife and others had always noted the "simmering impatience" he harbored. Eventually it was with great relief, even joy, that he realized "Oh, that's what I've been doing; that's why I've been so twisted up all the time" (his words).

Let's review the lies? First there were the superficial ones which he caught himself: 1) "I need to slap my wife; she's being so difficult". 2) My kids and my employees are getting worse, and I can't stand them anymore". The more substantial ones required a guide: 1) "I was fine until a few years ago; everything was great until I got irritable". 2) "I'm not scared;" this was a lie he told himself as a very young child and throughout his life. 3) "I know what happened to me;" no, he knew the factual content but had "forgotten" how painful it was, how scary. 4) "I'm over all that stuff about my parents and how they treated me".

These lies happened outside of Bully's awareness. He did not know what was motivating his behavior and his feelings, or even at first that something was wrong. He did not see himself becoming irritable, edgy, afraid, intolerant, verging on violent. At the time he knew only that he was "restless". Only when he slapped his wife did he begin to realize that there was more going on. Nor did he know, of course, what was causing the discomfort.

Once he did learn – and by "learn" I mean experienced at a gut level – his anxiety symptoms eased; he no longer needed to bully, he became more tolerant and less impatient, and he enjoyed his life again. He did not lose his ambition or his energy, but he did lose his dependence on them for his sense of security and self-esteem. He developed much greater intimacy with his wife and a whole new circle of friends. In my office I saw calmer, weightier presence, a grounded man; he became someone Morgan Freeman might play. Most important, he finally began to experience joy. This had never happened before. He would recount moments with his children, his friends, even at work, and his face would light up with a childlike pleasure that I had never seen him; he and his wife both told me that this was a new feeling for him. And by the way, this brought out another lie he had always told himself – "I love my life". In fact, he didn't, as his many symptoms and the reports from his family and friends showed. But he pushed all that aside (another lie). Only when his symptoms became severe enough for him to stop and notice them did he become aware that in fact he moved through his life with a tension similar to Claire's.

When psychotherapy stalls this kind of lie – that "I know what's going on, I know what this is about and I'm working on it" – may be the cause. Once identified, the therapy takes off again. 48-year-old Sandra came to see me on a high dose of antianxiety medication. When she was 10, her abusive alcoholic father left the family. She was thereafter raised by an increasingly hostile and unstable mother who shunned her, blamed her for almost everything, and meanwhile treated her younger brother like a Prince. During our time together, Sandra became calmer, less obsessively responsible for everything around her, less constantly and intensely apologetic and flinching, and – of most importance for her immediate ability to function – less enraged. Because of the internal pressure she constantly felt, she was prickly with others, quick to perceive accusation and unreasonable demands. This was a serious problem at work. She was in a service industry; part of her job was to deal with people who sometimes really were dumping their frustrations on her. She'd lost a job because she would respond defensively, and she was in danger of losing another when we met. Gradually she relaxed enough to perceive such stresses as nothing personal, as part of her job; she even got promoted.

But then we got stuck. She spoke constantly about the little improvements she made week by week, always harkening back to how she was raised, repeating variants on "because of how they treated me, I think I'm garbage and I'm always trying to fix that, that's how I act, I take on way too much blame, but I'm getting better; at least this time I managed to…" It was beginning to sound hollow to me, and in her clearer moments to her as well. But we couldn't seem to move forward until an episode in which she was arranging for a family gathering. Despite the terrible way her mother's side of the family always treated her, she felt an intense pressure to make all the travel arrangements, to pay for hotel rooms and airline fares in advance for these people. Worse, she felt compelled to do this despite past experience with many of them cancelling at the last minute and leaving her with the bills for the unused hotel rooms. She was well aware that any reasonable person's obligation in such a circumstance is limited to sending suggestions of places to stay, perhaps finding out if there is availability and what the prices are. But despite all of her supposed insight, she was being controlled by an irrational and self-destructive impulse. Why?

What Sandra was saying about her childhood was not a lie. She had correctly identified some lies that had dominated her life – that she was despicable, incompetent, and so on; that her maternal relatives' judgments of her were reasoned and warranted; that her brother was an angel; that it is her responsibility to fix any problem, anyone's discomfort, anything that occurs anywhere near her. She was not lying when she said that she had been improving. The lie was that there was nothing else going on. The lie was that she knew what was bothering her. If there was nothing else going on, if she knew what was wrong, she would not be struggling over that family gathering and the therapy would not have stalled.

One day we managed to interrupt her cycle of recounting the situation and reassuring herself with what she had learned thus far in therapy. She relaxed a bit and talked more spontaneously. It was then several memories came to mind from her childhood. In these memories, she was not picked on, pressured, guilty, shunned – or afraid of being shunned. She was terrified. In one of them, mother and father were in the front seat of the car, drunk, arguing, the two children in the back. As they sped along a busy thoroughfare, father suddenly threatened to swerve into the oncoming traffic and kill them all. Sandra remembered the scene vividly, how she tried to distract and comfort her little brother, how she stayed up all night prepared to call 911 while hearing her parents continue to argue, how she occasionally heard sounds that she feared were violence.

What Sandra did not remember until this session, what she'd "forgotten", was how scared she was, how helpless she felt. It was this terror that was fueling her obsessive concern with making arrangements for the family gathering. Proof of that can be seen in her reaction to remembering the terror. The obsessing disappeared! After a bout of tears in the office, she calmly decided to do "a little research for everyone", then to send options for accommodations and travel to the members of her family, but to do nothing more. She later told me they were grateful. No one in fact expected her to do more. So here, as with Bully, it was remembering the <u>experience</u> of key moments – not the content of those moments – that got her un-stuck and able to make decisions and move forward.

Here's a story of a family dinner that I heard from two of the participants. As the meal deteriorates, I hope you'll notice again the single mistake being made. In this family are a mother, father, and three children, ages 5, 7, and 12. This is an old-fashioned family in which father brought home the substantial bacon – they were well-off – and mother did everything else. She not only shielded father from all of the chaos, frustration, and endless detail of running the household and raising three children, but she developed a habit of complimenting and catering to father as if he were a teenager in need of praise and reassurance. One day, father came home from work in a shaky, irritated mood. Pressures were building up at work, he was having trouble with clients and colleagues, perhaps he feared for his previously secure standing, but in any case he came home feeling uncertain. At the dinner table, mother asked if he would speak to the gardener for her. The gardener was an old fart who believed women should be dutiful and silent; when she tried to remind him that they wanted this or that done, he'd grunt a dismissive acknowledgement but not actually comply. Preoccupied, father mumbled that he would handle it.

Mother sensed father's discomfort and fell into the routine of complimenting and reassuring him. She said "yes, you're so much better than I am at these things, I get all tongue tied, ruminating and furious; you know how to handle these people, you defuse the situation." As she did this, father became more distracted and tense – remember he wasn't feeling good in the first place and all of her praise now felt hollow. Seeing this, mother reflexively escalated her praise and chatter, her voice becoming more insistent. When the patriarch of the family is distressed, and when mother becomes distressed as well, you may rest assured the children sense it. The two younger ones began giggling and fiddling with their food; the teenager laughed a bit too loud, probably trying to distract himself and everyone from the tension at the table, and then opened his cell phone despite the family rule about that at the dinner table. In the midst of all this, father took his plate to the kitchen for seconds. Feeling bewildered and anxious as he left the room, mother snapped at the children after he was gone. The youngest child burst into tears, the middle one grinned nervously, staring down at his plate, the teenager continued to play with his cell phone. Dad reentered to this scene and barked "all right, everyone just sit down and eat, cell phones off, enough now!" The meal was finished in tense silence. At the end, the younger children were too upset to function – the seven-year-old couldn't focus on his homework, the five-year-old was whiny and demanding of attention, the teenager skipped his homework entirely and headed out aimlessly. Mother cleaned up dinner all the while nervously eating the left overs. A few months later her physician warned her that her cholesterol and blood pressure were becoming dangerously high, she was not sleeping enough, she looked older than her years, and that if she didn't find a way to decrease the stress in her life she was headed for a stroke or a heart attack in the near future.

Since this was the pattern of communication in this family, not a single event, any one of them could have end up in the therapist's office. Two did. And I honestly believe it could all be avoided if any of them but father in particular simply told the truth. If he had said out loud that he was having a bad day, that he was feeling shaky about things at work, mother would have been reassured. Even if she had lapsed into her usual litany of compliments, as long as father continued to tell the truth, saying "I know you think I'm brilliant sweetie, but actually here's what's going on…", she would have been reassured and this would have made all the difference. (Remember, I knew her.) Feeling heard, connected, and useful to her husband, she would have listened and perhaps even helped him sort out whatever was going wrong. It would have brought the two of them closer, easing both of their distress.

Children usually want to be part of such sane, loving, and productive communication, and the issue could thus have become a family moment. It might have bloomed into a nightly game of "who pissed you off today?" or "How did you handle a difficult person?" The children would have learned from this that difficult people and feeling shaky are part of life and – unlike Bully – would have grown up calmer, more forgiving of themselves and other people. The family might have laughed together about the gardener, perhaps agreed to fire him and do the work themselves, or made a group game of finding a nice gardener. Anything is possible and anything would've been better than what actually happened. Something else to notice about this dinner time is that everyone at the table needed reassurance and none of them asked for it or was even aware of it. Again, this is not a conscious lie. Probably no-one at the table, in the heat of the moment, noticed how needy they felt.

Finally, here's let's look at a couple. I have heard this story in slightly different versions so many times over the years, from so many different couples, both in my office and in my own life, that I present it here as an archetype. I'll call the parties "A" and "B", but be aware that I've heard this from gay couples, straight couples, young, old, rich, poor, educated and not.

A and B meet. A is attentive, charming, seductive. B flattered, warmed, excited, and returns the frothy, giddy attentiveness. Things progress. A gets less demonstrative for a while, perhaps preoccupied with problems at work, with A's mother or teenage daughter; perhaps it is simply the end of the courtship phase and A is relaxing. B panics but does not want to be whiny, needy, or in the one-down position, so B plays it cool, even if there are complaints made to sympathetic friends that A is unreliable, selfish, probably cheating. Meanwhile A senses something is wrong and tries to express concern or at least be more solicitous. B breezily dismisses A's concerns – if A expresses them out loud – trying to keep the atmosphere light. A is perplexed, possibly hurt, reaches out again, and perhaps B is reassured for a while. But both parties are now hypervigilant, scrutinizing and measuring every move, moment, action, and word for reassurance that all is well. In this tense atmosphere, momentary imperfections in their interaction cause the cycle to quickly repeat – B feeling slighted, A perplexed and hurt, neither speaking up about it.

One night in bed, A makes an advance. B politely declines, pleading back pain. Perhaps this is true, perhaps B is at that moment uncertain of A, perhaps resentful, perhaps just not in the mood. A tries to be a good egg and accept this, but in the context of their troubles is worried that B is drifting or no longer finds A attractive. Then A worries about worrying too much, about inventing problems, and so tries to accept that B is allowed to have moods. Still, A remains tense and uncertain. Pride rears its head and A begins to resent being in the position of "begging for it" and constantly worried about the relationship. In this prickly mood A is quick to feel slighted in other areas of life – at work, with friends, with the teenaged daughter who is having her own bad mood one day, with the daughter's dance teacher (true story) who wonders casually to A about whether A's daughter is still interested in lessons; she notes that the girl has not been practicing as much lately and perhaps could use a break. A takes offense, as if the teacher suggested A is not a good parent or that the child is an irresponsible brat. Eventually A's boss tells A to talk with someone about the irritability, about "being off your game".

A may come to see me worried about problems with anger, "stress", or just the boss' directive; or A may report a growing sense that everyone seems increasingly unsympathetic and unreasonable. B may come to see me worried about an impulse to have affairs just when someone has come along who might really be "the one". B may report that this has been a pattern in the past, ruining things just when they begin to look serious. Or B may tell us that this is the first time for such an impulse; that could indicate that this relationship is the most serious and therefore dangerous B has ever had; or it may mean that B is accurately perceiving A being either not as available as A seemed or that A is actually not "the one". Determining just what is going on with either A or B would require a lot of soul searching and a fair amount of checking in with past experiences. Both have to risk facing whatever emerges as true about each of them. Perhaps A would realize A is chronically inattentive and that being in a relationship will require more work; or A will have to accept that relationships are not a priority; or A may have to face a history of pulling away from people just when it gets interesting; perhaps A has a long history of profound self-doubt causing a dread that the ax will fall as soon as the defenses are down; perhaps A will realize A just plain likes being single and doesn't want to curtail any freedom. So many cans of worms might be opened – ye gods, it's so much easier to lie!

But how much better things would have been if A and B risked telling the truth? They might have gotten much closer, become best friends in addition to lovers, given each other all that we so hope for when we become involved. At worst, the relationship would have progressed much more quickly to its end, with a lot less confusion, frustration, wasted time, drama, and therapy bills.

You may wonder why I use the word "lie" so persistently. Surely no one in the five stories above means to lie. Everyone is probably trying to do their best. Certainly Claire's parents did not mean to lie to the child and of course they never wanted her to suffer as she was. Bully was trying his best to behave despite his chaotic feelings and did not want to lash out at his wife, children, or employees. A and B were no doubt trying to make their relationship work.

I use the word because it is jarring. As I said at the end of the Introduction, my goal here is clarity. I don't want to say anything that diffuses the message. When you call something a misunderstanding, a confusion, a distortion, or anything else, you've watered down the impact and at worst confused the issue – lied about it. I intentionally use the word "lie" to shake off complacency and heighten your vigilance. Also, when lies are uncovered – as you can see in just the few cases we've looked at so far – the impact is powerful. It deserves a strong word like "lie". That intense reaction we saw in Bully, Sandra, Claire when the lies were exposed is not the response of someone who broke through a "misunderstanding".

(There is precedent for my concern with using a strong, evocative word. In translating him into English, the Standard Edition of Freud's complete works criminally watered down his language, stripping it of all its original impact. For example, his term "id" was originally the German word for "It". "Id" was taken from the Latin and has no real resonance; for most of us it's a made up term. "It" is something quite different – there have been horror movies with that title. "It" calls up all the spooky deep unknown that Freud wanted to invoke by so naming this dark, chaotic, and unconscious area of the psyche. The same is true of "ego" – Freud's word for that was "the I". My favorite example is the description of dreams. Freud said they were a manifestation of activity of the "seele", German for "soul". Think about that word, "soul". What does it conjure up for you? Everything in your deepest heart, everything you love/hate/fear the most? In the American translation that phrase became "Dreams are a manifestation of mental activity", which is about as informative as saying walking is a manifestation of leg activity.*[2])

We start lying to ourselves early in life, usually in order to survive. Very quickly we start believing the lies, the ones we are told (like Sandra and Claire), and the ones we tell ourselves so we can function (Bully and Sandra saying "I know what happened; I'm handling it"). When this happens early enough and is not corrected by other experiences, the result can be an entire life pulled off track, as we saw with Bully and Sandra. In such cases, it can take a lot of work – usually in psychotherapy – to put things right, to get your life back.

Unfortunately it's just so damned easy to lie. Children approaching puberty start with the bravado of "I don't care", "I ain't scared", and some soon believe it. Children growing up under the spell of such lies end up like Bully, Sandra or the many others I'll be talking about. This is why "parental alienation" is so destructive and is classified as child abuse. Parental alienation occurs in custody/visitation disputes between parents; it is a conscious lie. One parent tries to prejudice – poison – the child

---

[2]   For more on these appalling mistranslations, have a look at *Freud and Man's Soul* by Bruno Bettelheim, published in 1982.

against the other. When the message from the alienator is at odds with external reality – when the alienated parent is in fact a good parent with a previously strong relationship with the child – the results can be serious for the child. Research has consistently shown that the kids swayed by such efforts have many more adjustment problems then kids going through custody/visitation battles without parental alienation. They often have more trouble in school, with peers, with authority, with depression, with self-esteem, with behavior, with everything.

Even high functioning adults, without an agenda like a parent in a custody dispute, fall with remarkable ease into lying. My father – and thanks, Dad, for your permission to tell this story – gave a perfect demonstration of this. About 30 years ago I was passing through the town in which he lived and I needed to park my dog somewhere for a couple of hours. I asked him if I could leave the hound up tied up in the back yard for the duration; he'd never even have to see the animal. My father's answer was a reflexive and impatient "What do I want a dog for?" in a tone of "that's the stupidest question I've ever been asked". Now bear in mind, my father doesn't think I'm stupid, almost always wants to help, didn't think the question was stupid, doesn't usually attack people, and knew I wasn't offering him a dog. So a true answer would've been something like "sorry, kiddo, but I really don't want a dog here; maybe you can ask someone else?"

So why did he lie? Largely because he loves me and did not want to say "no". It might make him feel like a bad father, might make him worry that I'll be disappointed or even angry with him. He was in his sixties at the time, I was the youngest of four and the last to leave home, and like most parents he was often wishing I'd come around more often; so he could have been be particularly worried about any upset I might feel at his refusing me. We could even speculate that, again unconsciously, he avoided directly declining my request because it might stir up other uncomfortable feelings about being tired of the burden; he'd had three decades by then of paying for tennis lessons, summer camps, music lessons, dentists, braces, colleges, etc., three decades of attending bad school concerts (he came to all my plays) and little league games. No parent wants to feel resentful of or burdened by their children, even though it's not an unreasonable feeling at times. In any event, whatever the reasons, my father reflexively pushed all the discomfort that my question raised in him back onto me by answering me as if I had said something preposterous.

Why is this important? Because this kind of casual lie gets us lost and stuck. There are people who habitually talk as my father did to me for that moment; then they wonder why they are unpopular, lonely, can't hold a job. Looking at the receiving end, had I been built like Sandra you can imagine how always hearing this kind of attitude from a parent would greatly contribute to a chronic anxiety and belief that whatever I do or say is stupid and wrong. And, also like Sandra, I might struggle with chronic rage at being made to feel so stupid and wrong; being extra sensitive to such treatment, I might be extremely quick to feel insulted, quick to argue and defend, not an easy person to work with or love.

These are common outcomes, not hypotheticals; people do get lost in this way. Carl announced to me in his first sessions, and for a good year thereafter, that he needed to figure out how to be a better person so that his wife would love him. This sounds like a noble undertaking, particularly if he'd been a recovering addict, a chronic womanizer, violent, or just habitually thoughtless. Once we began talking, however, I couldn't find anything to fix! His treatment of his wife, his handling of business associates and clients, his relationships with friends, his parenting of his young children, his self-discipline, his balance of work and other activities, all were exemplary. Eventually it emerged that Carl's wife had 10 years earlier announced that she did not love him and was not attracted to him, although she was attracted to other men. This message had not changed in the intervening decade. Moreover, their entire relationship was only 12 years old and for the first year was conducted long-distance; they only saw each other about one weekend a month.

Here were the lies that eventually surfaced in Carl. 1) "We had a great relationship." 2) "As soon as I figure out how to better myself, what

I'm doing wrong, we'll have that great relationship again." 3) "I've never been horrifically alone or abandoned in my life by anyone, except when it was my fault, and I can fix that if you help me figure out what's wrong with me." 4) "I'm not angry about any of this."

It turned out that Carl grew up with a remarkably uninvolved and uninterested father. He was often away on business and when home showed absolutely no support for or interest in anything about Carl except that the boy might become a businessman. Throughout his childhood, Carl showed artistic and creative gifts. He was particularly interested in architecture, for which he received much praise and encouragement from teachers and eventually recommendations for advanced training and a career. Carl's father refused to pay for anything but business school, despite the family's substantial means. Carl's mother was "flaky and intense", hyperbolic in her praise of him but easily overwhelmed by the slightest stress. So especially when Carl was a child and subject to the normal neediness of a person that age, she was quick to throw up her hands in despair and run tearfully to her room.

For whatever reason, Carl's adaptation to all this was to become the family glue. He ran from parent to parent, always reassuring them – and reassuring himself that he had not been abandoned. Other children adapt differently; this was Carl's way. Very quickly this became his *modus operandi*, the lens through which he viewed and lived his life. He vividly recalled being quite popular in grade school yet fixated on the one boy who did not respond to him. By the time I met him, he was living out this same pattern with his wife. Despite all the others who responded to him, he endlessly pursued this woman who had really never been available to him. He agonized over how to mend their relationship, taking on the entire burden of this task himself, just as he did as a child with his parents. As he couldn't then, he still was unable to demand that the other people in relationships with him hold up their end. Also as he did in younger years he let drop all his own interests and passions. It was no surprise to hear that he suffered from poor sleep and bouts of agitated worry. We might also notice that his career path was another reenactment of his childhood. When I met him he was in upper management in a large corporation and his job was largely to oil the workings within and between teams; once again he was the family glue.

Why does Carl lie about – ignore – all this and instead maintain the fantasy that all will be well as soon as he fixes himself and thereby his marriage? Because painful as it is to continue in his frantic scramble to figure out what's wrong with him and keep everyone else's life well oiled, the scramble protects him from the following painful realities: 1) My wife doesn't love me and hasn't for most of the time I have known her; 2) this experience is a repetition of an even more agonizing one from childhood, when I was more painfully and frighteningly abandoned; 3) in childhood, in my marriage, perhaps other times in between, I have spent a great deal of emotional energy chasing unavailable people at the expense of my own life, joys, passions, fulfillment; 4) facing all this may well bring despair, rage, sorrow which at times will feel crushing.

Romantic relationships are particularly fertile soil for lies. We saw how easily couples fall into it in the example of "A" and "B" above. Here are some common lies which are particularly damaging. Again, bear in mind that they are usually unconscious.

"We love and need each other equally". The problem here is that we so want and need this to be true because it usually piggybacks on another lie: "My worth, value, almost my right to be, are threatened by the humiliation or failure involved in being the one less loved, the more needy one". And because we don't acknowledge that these are our feelings – because we lie to ourselves and each other – we compensate in all kinds of destructive ways. Most frequent is the hyper-scrutiny we saw between A and B. A close second is the defensive retreat from that intensity, into a dismissive, "cool" attitude that we saw B trying to adopt. In either case, the relationship can become suffused with pressure, resentment, tension; nothing kills a romance faster. Of all the times men have come to my office for a consultation about their sexual performance, the problem has almost never been sexual. Instead we almost always find that the organs and desire work just fine but the act has been ruined by anger, resentment, or the pressure to perform – not just sexually but in every word and deed.

One frequent lie (written about in the 2008 novel *Olive Kitteridge* by Elizabeth Strout) is more difficult to give up: "When I'm married, or in a relationship, I will finally have enough of the attention and reassurance that I think I need – enough praise, e-mails, texts, phone calls, cards, flowers, sex – so that I will no longer feel alone, uncertain, shaky, or anything else unpleasant that I've felt in the past." Of course, it is very rare that a relationship can provide all that and few of us can function in a relationship with that kind of pressure. Sex is the least of the problems when there is that much riding on every moment. When the relationship fails to perform as we fantasize, then comes the resentment, insecurity, yearning, sorrow, accusation, or just withdrawal.

Surveys have shown that couples delay an average of six years from the time they first sense problems until they seek help. Bear in mind that that's six years from when <u>they</u> see a problem; friends and family may have noticed it earlier. By the time they do reach out, they are sometimes in the state which a mentor of mine who specializes in couples work calls "fused". They do not view each other as separate beings anymore but rather – and again this happens unconsciously – as mirrors of validation or frustration.

In a very high functioning, compassionate, warm, married couple I saw, the wife said in session that she had thought about suicide a few times over the years. Her husband's response was to gaze into the middle distance, not looking at me or at her, and to say almost to himself "damn, you never told me"; then he was silent. He was consumed by feeling left out, invalidated, and he hardly noticed his wife as a separate creature in pain. For her part, the wife was similarly fused. She did not notice how lonely and desolate her husband's response left her, ironic because such moments between them over the years probably contributed to her suicidal thoughts in the first place.

Here's another example of a fused couple. Fred was stepping into his first professional audition after a few years of amateur theater, where he'd met Karen, a successful fundraiser high up in the corporate world. The evening after the audition, they met for dinner and Karen naturally asked how it went. Fred gushed, only briefly, with astonishment at how well he had done and how many companies had asked to see him for a second audition. Then he spent the rest of the evening and the following week in a state of agitated obsessing over every trivial detail of his life – what time he would go to sleep that evening in order to get up for work, whether he would go to the hardware store the next day or the pharmacy first, whether he wanted to go hiking the next Saturday or put it off until Sunday, etc. etc. Why did this happen?

Fred told me this story about two years later, when he first came to see me. He presented it to illustrate of one of his main symptoms – chronic worry and obsessing that often seemed to come out of nowhere and which greatly constricted his life, his focus, his ability to experience anything beyond anxiety. It turns out that Fred was lying to himself in his recounting of the story. Eventually I found out what really happened – and I was later able to confirm this with Karen. When Fred answered her question about his audition her eyes drifted down and to the side, her smile became forced and oddly sad, and then she changed the subject. Fred edited this part of the story out of his memory because of his own personality quirks. Perhaps you or I might respond in such a situation by saying "hello? Is something wrong? This is exciting news I'm sharing." Fred, however, was similar to Carl and Sandra; he grew up always blaming himself for any negative feelings and for any moment of disconnection from another person. His father talked to him constantly as my father did to me in that moment with the dog. This is partly why Fred always thought that if someone like Karen looked bored or uncomfortable it must be because Fred was doing something wrong, and that he should immediately stop and figure out what's wrong with him. Hence the automatic, habitual retreat into worry and obsessing, which is the symptom that brought him into my office.

This was a particularly easy trap for Fred because Karen was ordinarily such a responsive and supportive girlfriend. It seemed to him out of character for her to respond as she did. But again Fred was distorting things in his memory – lying to himself – by "forgetting" the many previous occasions in which Karen pulled away oddly and he was left feeling similarly shaken; he eventually remembered how any time he had a success – maybe just telling a successful joke at a party – she would become at least subtly withholding and distant. (Gradually he noticed a direct correlation between his moments of success and her cold withdrawal; the greater the former, the more obvious and abrupt the latter.)

It turns out that Karen, too, grew up with a chronic shakiness deep in her core; she especially struggled with a lot of painful sibling rivalry. When Fred shared his triumph with her, a deep sense of inadequacy and competitiveness arose in her. She usually kept such feelings at bay but, as always happens in our close relationships, her defenses were weaker with Fred and so out came the primitive anxieties. She lied – to herself and therefore then to Fred – in not noticing them, and then by changing the subject so lightly and dismissively as if, to Fred's anxious eyes, without a care in the world. I like the image here of skipping stones on a lake. Instinctively, protectively, and rapidly we bounce off of our unpleasant feelings unless we're vigilant; you can see that's what my father did.

By contrast, imagine how close, warm, loved, connected, and reassured these two might have felt that moment and for the rest of the evening had they been able to tell the truth to each other. I know Fred. The last thing he would have been is unsympathetic to Karen's inner demons. And having heard the truth from her, he would have been greatly nourished and relieved by the discovery that her withdrawal was not a sign that something is wrong with him, as he habitually believed; on the contrary, he would have seen that she responded so oddly because there is <u>not</u> something wrong with him and because he matters so much to her.

Finally, we should not move on without brief mention of perhaps the most destructive lie people tell each themselves in relationships: "Next time this will work". How many relationships drag on in sour repetition because one or both parties try the same tactic to convince or change the other, even though it has never worked? Most painfully, this is the lie you often hear from couples in violent relationships. "Next time I'll finally get through, he'll understand (or she will) and it will be different". Incidentally, this is the same thing substance abusers are often telling themselves, sometimes not even unconsciously, before they turn around; "the next high will finally be enough."

We seem to need lies. Too many times I have read accounts in the *New York Times* or the *Wall Street Journal* of something I either witnessed or participated in, and found that I scarcely recognized the event. It had been tarted up to make a good story, given a good humorous buildup and punchline, or treated with reverence that wasn't there, or given a zing that it didn't have. I've seen thoughtful, observant people do this. I suspect, at least in my less cynical moments, that the writers of those stories were not always aware of altering them in the telling; that is, I think they were unconsciously distorting things. The playwright and performer Alan Bennett was talking on camera about Sir Alec Guinness the actor, and he said that "what strikes me is that there's never been a convincing imitation of him". In that same documentary on Guinness, the author John le Carré did a priceless and dead on impression. When a cast member of *Star Trek: The Next Generation* took over the direction of one of the movies, Patrick Stewart who plays the captain talked enthusiastically in an interview about how there has to be a *Star Trek* veteran at the helm to do a successful *Star Trek* movie. Two of the *Star Trek* movies that were the greatest critical and popular successes were written and directed by Nicholas Meyer, a Shakespeare scholar who at the time had never even seen *Star Trek*. I mention these stories because I do not believe that the people involved are stupid, reckless, or unreasonable. Yet the lies come so naturally! The celebrated novelist Saul Bellow wrote in one of his most famous books (*The Adventures of Augie March*, 1953) "One day's ordinary falsehood if you could convert it into silt would choke the Amazon back a hundred miles over the banks".

This is a good time to pause and emphasize that I am not excluding myself from any of this. It's taken decades to identify and root out the lies in my own life. I'd like to think I've caught most of them, but it won't surprise me if I'm wrong. It won't surprise me if in in 10 years I look back and again shake my head at how full of it I've been.

Lying starts early, earlier than Sandra, Bully, Carl remember. Imagine a child about 8 months old who reaches for and points to things around him, as is the habit of a child of that age. His mother is anxious. Maybe she always is, maybe this is her first child, maybe it's her third child in as many years and she's getting fed up, maybe her husband just left her, maybe she just left him, whatever. In any event, she barks anxiously at her child, in a voice too loud and strident, while rushing over to whisk him into his high chair for safety.

Now assume that this is not a single occasion of mom's bad mood, but a regular occurrence – better yet, let's assume it's an inconsistent occurrence, dependent upon the whims of her mood. Does the child say to himself, "Ah, well, Mom's uptight. I mustn't take this personally. I can explore the world later when she's calm or when she's not around." Impossible. He's barely a year old. He can't put mother's behavior into this kind of adult perspective. Instead he learns that this is the way of the universe: Small actions on his part unpredictably lead to catastrophic reactions. Remember that mother's outburst might be only a mild irritant to another adult, but to a small child it is a frightening assault, especially coming from the person on whom the child is most dependent for all physical and emotional sustenance.

Always expecting a blow to fall, an explosion of anxiety and displeasure, a criticism, a censure, he could grow into a "flincher" – one of those people who is endlessly apologizing, timid, and tense. Alternatively, he might grow up battling that same anxiety – the humiliation and trauma of so displeasing the one on whom he is most dependent – by blustering his way through the world as if such experiences could never happen again. Such is the bully, the braggart. Another possibility is that he becomes one of those super-competent, always-in-the-know people, and in that way forever avoids the catastrophic anxiety and consequences of doing the wrong thing. There are other possible adaptations. Whether any of them are successful depends upon a lot of other things – intelligence, flexibility of other defenses, ability to choose people and environments that reward such personalities, etc. But whatever the eventual adaptation, the child still grows up constantly fleeing or fighting off the horror of that parental upset, as Bully, Carl, and Sandra realized they were doing. This kind of outcome is especially likely if a child's genetic makeup is one of high sensitivity, making him particularly attuned to his mother's moods and fearful of her outbursts.

The lie here is one of the earliest, and it's the one we saw most clearly in Bully and Sandra: "I'm not overwhelmed and terrified by this". The flincher may appear at first glance to be free of this lie, but he is lying too (again, unconsciously). He lies by flinching at everything else in the world, things that don't warrant such avoidance and anxiety, while not remembering what really scared him and how bad that felt. Ron, a patient I'll be discussing in detail later, gave a wonderful example of this kind of displaced flinching. A highly successful, socially adept and attractive young man, not a womanizer, he had recently separated quite amicably and by mutual consent from a sweet and calm woman he'd been dating for a few months. As he crossed the street to my office, he found himself having almost shaking with anxiety over a fantasy that this woman would any moment emerge around a nearby corner hauling a large Gatling gun and blast him to shreds with it. You may not be surprised to learn that Ron grew up the victim of unpredictable and as he remembers it even gleefully administered physical abuse, which he described to me but no longer remembered on a gut level; as he once put it, "it's kind of like I'm remembering someone else's life when I think about it."

Perhaps because lies are so destructive and so prevalent, the truth seems to be a passion in our species. Our earliest documents date back about 5000 years and they tend to be rather dull – deeds of land ownership, statements of finances. Our oldest profession appears to have been bookkeeping or lawyering. Most of us know what the second oldest profession is. The third oldest profession, at least from the written records appears to be what were later called philosophers and scientists. Very quickly, as soon as any society stabilized to the point that people did not have to fight off predators or hunt for food each day, a group of people begin to spend their time thinking and writing about the questions of what is real, what is true. Topics include the world around them, the weather, the stars, human behavior, why people go to war, why things live and die, the nature of human existence.

In my profession Cognitive Behavioral Therapy has been for the past 20 years or so one of the most talked about of the treatments. As any of you know who are familiar with it, the focus is on uncovering and challenging the lies we have come to believe – if I don't do well in that presentation I'll be fired, if I stumble during the presentation I'll be laughed at and humiliated and unable to ever show my face again, if that girl doesn't go out with me I'll be crushed and never able to show my face again, if I get into that airplane I'll panic and die, …. "Mindfulness" is a more recent trend. Again, if you really look at it, the goal is catching the lies. Mindful eating, for example, is a process of greatly slowing down and focusing on eating without any distractions. The result is that the eater is forced to notice – not lie about – what is happening to him, perhaps that he full but still eating because he's angry, anxious, lonely, bored, emotionally "empty", and so on.

Some of the film actors who so capture our attention are doing so, I believe, because of this power to identify truth and then share it with us. Lines like "you can't handle the truth!" (Jack Nicholson in *A Few Good Men*), or "just when I thought I was out they pull me back in" (Al Pacino in *Godfather 3*) are not brilliant lines, but they capture our imagination because of the delivery. Somehow these actors make us sit forward and lean into the screen, and later we remember and savor the lines as we strive to grasp every whiff of the truth we heard in them. The same is probably true in other arts, in Edvard Munch's painting "The Scream" or Magritte's "Le Viol" ("The Rape"). I believe these artists have captured a truth about how we feel at least sometimes, and that truth is deeply compelling. Bruce Lee the martial artist said late in his life that his great goal in his work was not to do something "impressive, to make your jaw drop", but "to do something honest". His word.

I've always loved the movies and two that best capture the process of psychotherapy are *Good Will Hunting* (1997), and *Ordinary People* (1980). In each of these a boy is healed when he learns that he has been lying to himself about what he feels. And each boy resists most strongly that which he most needs to learn. You may remember the climactic scene in *Good Will Hunting* when Robin Williams as the therapist keeps repeating to the boy, referring to his long history of physical abuse by his father, "it wasn't your fault". The boy repeatedly shrugs off this reassurance saying "I know" until he first rages and then breaks down in passionate tears because in fact he <u>didn't</u> know. He had been lying to himself that he knew it wasn't his fault, that he knew his father was a worthless slob. What was poisoning his life – making him for all his bravado unable to take risks, unable to enjoy his many gifts and interests – was his deeper belief that it <u>was</u> his fault, that he was worthless. These are Hollywood movies so the therapy is telescoped into a few key moments and the cure comes in a few dramatic sessions, but otherwise the depiction is accurate. People resist learning exactly that which is most personal and would most free them, what they most need to know. And when we break through that resistance and reveal the lies, that's when therapy and life take off.

When I was writing this book, my editor pressed me to break down the process of identifying the lies in one's life into clear steps. Even if you've haven't seen the two movies I just discussed, perhaps you already understand why I was reluctant to do this. Each person's route out of the lies in their life is going to be different. In *Good Will Hunting*, the boy was in touch with his rage but not with how unsure he was of himself. In *Ordinary People*, the boy starts off painfully insecure and only late in the movie discovers how furious he is. Each had to learn what the other already knew, although in both cases, the discovery frees them from their misery and from their isolated, inhibited, and constricted lives.

Still, with that caveat in mind, I will offer a few suggestions about how to get started. In order to catch yourself lying you may first have to do something first that is very un-American: Slow down, breathe, step back. Think of the examples from early in this chapter of Karen, the couple A and B, and the family dinner. You can see it would be hard for anyone in these vignettes to stop in the heat of the moment and ask himself "why my doing this, this isn't what I really mean to do/say, what's going on here?" Such stopping and stepping back may even be counter to our DNA, especially us males. When we were living in caves some 4 million years ago, he who hesitated got eaten by the tiger or didn't catch the antelope. Those of us alive now may descend from creatures naturally selected for their tendency to take action.

Something else you can do is take an interest in lies. Notice when you or anyone else oddly change the subject, as Karen did when she got uncomfortable during her dinner with Fred, as Fred did in response to Karen's perplexing turn-away. Catch the tendency to shrug off something you feel or perceive with that easy "oh that's silly; why would I feel/do/say/think that?" The cases of Greg in chapter 5 and Evan at the top of chapter 6 are good illustrations of this kind of resistance.

It's easiest to see lies in other people, hardest to see them in ourselves. So take the easier route and watch what goes on around you. Notice the small moments, especially with people you aren't close to so you'll be more objective. Take an interest in that curiously exhilarating or depressing or irritating brief encounter you had at the local coffee shop. Take note of when something feels forced, hollow, or otherwise "off". Chances are it's because someone is not telling the truth, because something in their words, demeanor, actions, tone of voice rings false. And watch out for hearing yourself saying what Sandra, Bully, the boy in *Good Will Hunting*, and so many others say: "Yeh, I know already; I know what happened to me, I know what I feel, I know why I feel this way, I know what I'm doing". If we really knew all that we wouldn't be having any symptoms. If that statement seems a stretch right now, hang on for a chapter or two and I'm confident you'll be convinced.

Here's a particularly hard one. Resist the temptation to get defensive. Even if someone is intrusively and inappropriately diagnosing you, give yourself the chance to try on what they're saying. I know a woman whose boyfriend suggested that her cheerful and superficially friendly behavior towards a busy bartender was not as it seemed. She kept interrupting the bartender with jokes and questions just at the moments when he was doing three things at once and had his back turned. This woman was ordinarily quite sensitive and socially graceful, so something other than a basic cluelessness must have been operating. Her boyfriend shared these observations with her. Unlike most people she was able to say to herself "hey, that's true; I <u>am</u> bothering this busy guy; I know how to chat with a bartender without being a pest, what's going on with me here?"

As soon as she did this, she told me, the answer was obvious. The first thing she realized is that she was quite tense and eager to please. The next thing she realized was that she hadn't realized this; instead, she was overcompensating with a boisterous bonhomie in hopes of impressing her new boyfriend, and perhaps other people. Why is this discovery important? Because it opened her up to the realization that she carried a great deal of tension around to which she was often oblivious but which pushed away the very people she wanted to impress. Second, it led to a greater intimacy with her boyfriend. Most important, it calmed her. As soon as one sees and accepts that one is tense – as soon as one stops lying about it – one is no longer controlled by it.

You may need a guide. This is especially true if your life has gotten as far derailed as was Bully's, Sandra's, and Carl's, or if you and your partner inadvertently poke right into each other's hangups the way Fred and Karen did. Don't be discouraged by this. People benefit from even three or four sessions of psychotherapy. Not everybody stays for years.

Especially you couples, catch the lies early. Catch them young. Don't wait until tension has been building for a decade. Take an interest in the small moments. Don't brush them under the carpet saying "I didn't want to rock the boat" and then wait 10 years to address them, as Fred did. The boat's already rocked.

Our story so far: Lies happen a lot, they happen very easily, they can start very young, and they get us lost and stuck, causing a great deal of misery and constriction in our lives. The cure is to expose them, to bring them into consciousness. Getting un-lost and un-stuck is the obvious reason to catch the lies, but there's another. As we saw in Bully, as we'll see in future cases I'll describe, there's a further benefit which one of my patients expressed beautifully. He called to resume our work after a brief hiatus and told me this about his reason for returning: "It's not just the relief from my anxiety. Life gets so much bigger! I see how different I can be, how much there is to enjoy as opposed to walking around tense and defensive and not even realizing it. There's a whole new way to move through the world, to experience things, to be with people, to be with myself. It's wild!"

CHAPTER 2

LYING AND WHY PSYCHOTHERAPY

I've said that identifying and rooting out the lies in our lives is the cure for a lot of our unhappiness. In my experience, this cure happens mostly in psychotherapy, but there are other ways to break through lies. Good yoga classes, encounter sessions, intensive weekend workshops, good relationships, even acting classes can all contribute. But psychotherapy has, I believe, the best chance at exposing the substantial lies that poison our lives, so that's what I'll be focusing on as we go. In the process, I'll be describing in much more detail than in the last chapter how personality forms, how defenses and symptoms come about, how lies invade and then permeate our lives, and how psychotherapy works – what should happen in it, how to know if it's working, when to go, when to stop.

Psychotherapy and its practitioners have always been favorite objects of merciless lampooning, right up there with accountants and morticians. Just about every television comedy ever aired has at least one episode where some incompetent or bizarre therapist is the source of the laughs. In the real world, psychotherapy is maligned and devalued, both by outsiders and from within the field itself. Despite occasional trendiness, seeing a therapist is still tinged with negative stigma: If you see a shrink, you must be crazy or weak or lonely or gullible or whatever. And finally, yes there are many incompetent therapists doing business and they don't help this image.

Amid all that, it can be very difficult to make an informed decision about psychotherapy for yourself or someone close to you. Questions about the subject are met with a barrage of conflicting opinions: Should I go? Should my child go? Should I and my spouse or current companion go? Can it help? Is it worth the expense? Who should I see? How do

I choose among therapists and therapies? How long will it take? What will happen in sessions? Just what is psychotherapy anyway? What does it do and what's it good for? And why can't I get the help I need from a book or a friend (or a yoga class, or an acting class)? If you are already in treatment, you may have other questions: Is it helping, and how can I tell? How can I tell if my therapist knows what he's doing? When should I stop going?

I will address each of these questions and more, in some detail, in the chapters that follow. By the end of the book, you will understand how psychotherapy frees you from the lies, how it works, what it is and what it isn't — there are a lot of misconceptions — when to go, when to stop. You will see, as we've started to, how people get lost and stuck in the first place, how the lies happen. You will see why self-help books, lectures, workshops, acting and yoga classes, even wise and patient friends often cannot help, and why some treatments go on for years while others are over in a few months.

You'll also see, as I've tried to show in the vignettes I've already presented, that psychotherapy is not some esoteric, undefinable, even mystical process. It is not a faith to which only the converts adhere. It is a logical, discernible process that anyone can understand and follow, whose benefits or failures are apparent to all. In psychotherapy, you need not accept your therapist's strange ideas without skepticism and questioning. On the contrary, in good psychotherapy every step should make complete sense to the patient; you may end up in strange territory, but it should be entirely clear how you got there. There is no reason for anything in a psychotherapy session to be unreasonable or mysterious. This last point I will continue to emphasize and illustrate throughout this book. By the end, you should be able to grade your therapist's work as well as any colleague or licensing body.

A person looks to psychotherapy because he is lost or stuck. He may feel this way or it may be evident in his behavior, but in any case that is the problem. It is in fact the problem whether the patient presents with anxiety, depression, panic, phobias, obsessive-compulsive disorder (OCD), post-traumatic stress, adolescent rebellion, drug abuse, separation anxiety, wife beating, compulsive promiscuity, or almost anything else. This may seem an extreme statement, but bear with me a while. As to the objection that there is a chemical basis to depression, OCD, etc., remember that brain chemistry is known to change in concert with a very wide variety of experiences, right down to hearing music or seeing a traffic light. Whether and to what degree the change in chemistry is cause or effect of mood change remains unclear, as are the specifics of those brain chemistry changes; we know Prosac increases the amount of serotonin floating around in the nervous system, but we don't really know what else it does or what else makes the depressed person depressed.

When a person enters psychotherapy, or is dragged into it by others, the common element among all the above presenting problems is that his behavior, feelings, thoughts, perceptions seem irrational. We, and he, cannot understand why he feels so angry, so depressed, so obsessed with triviality, so afraid of nothing. He says he is worthless, he believes he is hated, he believes the government has labeled him a terrorist and that he must hide, he is sure no woman could ever care for him, he is sure that all women love him.

He may be ruining his life with drugs or alcohol despite his own desire to stop. Or he washes his hands until they are raw, all the while knowing that this is pointless and self-destructive. He beats his wife or girlfriend, yet is sure that he loves her; perhaps he does. He constantly alienates people with his arrogant and supercilious attitude, ruining his chances for social and professional success, yet he is the first one to see such self-destructive patterns in others. He gets into one masochistic relationship after another, each time suffering the abuse and insensitivity of his lover and swearing never to make that mistake again. He breaks into a cold sweat, his heart races, and he is sick with fear when he gets into a crowded elevator, yet he knows all the statistics about how safe elevators are and that he is in fact in greater real danger sitting in his bathtub.

These people have lost track of something in themselves that is now driving their apparently irrational behavior, feelings, point of view; there's a lie going on. They may know they are unhappy, often they are more than smart enough to understand that their behavior isn't working for them anymore, but for some reason they can't change. There is some other motivation, agenda, feeling, which is drawing them into these repeated patterns. <u>When they make contact with that other agenda, when the lie is exposed, they begin to change</u>. Meanwhile, they have lost themselves and remain stuck in unproductive, unsatisfying, or self-destructive patterns of behavior.

The same applies to couples who cannot understand their squabbling, even to children and adolescents who may claim to enjoy their misbehavior. Somehow, there are hidden agendas causing behavior and feelings that don't seem to make sense. The adolescent who gets high all the time can usually understand that this behavior will get him nowhere he wants to be in life (although you usually can't get him to admit that out loud); the class clown may want the kids to laugh, but usually wants the teacher to like him as well; the school phobic child does want to join the other kids in school. But these people have lost track of themselves in some way. Desires, needs, motives, even thoughts and ideas, lurk just out of awareness, and they are influencing these persons' behavior and feelings.

So with these questions – these symptoms of being lost and/or stuck – a person calls a therapist. He says "Why is this happening? Why do I do what I do, when I know I don't want to?"

Taking this idea of being lost one step further, in fact many people enter psychotherapy not even knowing what symptoms they really have. I made that point in the last chapter about men who have consulted me for possible sexual dysfunction. The same is true of Attention Deficit Disorder. This has been a very popular label. Children are frequently brought in with this diagnosis on their school records or on the minds of their parents; a few years back there was a spate of adults calling me to say they'd been diagnosed with "Adult ADD". Again, perhaps 1 out of 8 such referrals is a true case of attention deficit. Instead the problem usually turns out to be an something going on between the child and specific authority figures, a case of separation anxiety, reaction to family turmoil, or something else in the emotional arena. Ironically, the most glaring case I ever saw of this disorder had gone undiagnosed for all 17 years of the boy's life. When he finally saw a psychiatrist who specializes in attention deficit, this colleague told me it was one of the clearest and easiest diagnoses he ever made.

If you think about it, being lost means almost certainly that in fact you do <u>not</u> know what is wrong. If you did, you might not need psychotherapy. A case example: Tom came to see me complaining of an elevator phobia. It turned out that the symptom originated in large office buildings where he was forced to ask creditors for extensions of loans, bankers for more money to build his business, etc. For a while afterwards, he suffered little anxiety while riding elevators to a friend's apartment or a rooftop restaurant but soon these became phobic experiences as well.

Initially we talked about some ways to cope with the phobia when it arose, or threatened to. He gave a stab at these methods with some success, but then began reporting other problems including panic and a constant feeling of pressure and frustration. After about 5 sessions, we began to discuss what happened to him before and during the kind of business meeting where the problems seemed to have started. With a certain amount of cheerleading from me, since he was not a man given to talking about feelings, he described the humiliation and rage he felt but usually kept "tucked away where I don't think about it." To his surprise, he became quite emotional in the telling. The next week he came in and told me the phobia was greatly diminished. He rode elevators all week with only a few brief episodes of anxiety. What happened?

This man's "phobia" really had to do with a fear of confrontation and of being in what he perceived as a humiliating position, such as asking others for money. He was lost with regard to what hurt. He thought he was scared of elevators; in fact he was scared of certain people in certain contexts. Had he known this, he might well have gotten over the phobia himself. In any case, once the true issues came into awareness, the original phobia lost its power and simply evaporated. Treatment continued for another few months. I spoke to Tom about 3 years later and he told me his phobic symptoms had not recurred.

Tom's is of course a particularly straightforward case, but it is not unusual to see this kind of immediate symptom relief following simply the identification of the problem, exposure of the lie. Here is a more extended illustration of this process.

George came in complaining of memory problems. At the age of 56, he was worried he might be growing senile. Medically, there was no evidence for any of this, however brain scans cannot detect Alzheimer's or certain other causes of senility so George remained worried. As I talked to this man, I found myself getting oddly irritated. In reviewing just when in session this happened, I began to suspect that George was retreating into "memory problems" to avoid things – a discussion, feeling, encounter, or person that made him uncomfortable. If so, this is an irritation I know well. It comes when I have the vague and barely conscious sense of being controlled. (I'm lying to myself with this "irritation" because in fact what I'm really feeling at such times – under the macho nonsense – is hurt, ignored, stepped on, stepped over, insignificant, and enraged about all that.) By adopting this helpless stance of memory loss, George in effect controls the conversation and avoids whatever is confronting him, including me. He even demands my sympathy with this stance. He was not conscious of doing this, of course; if he had been, he could simply stop.

Sounds interesting, but how do we know any of this is true? I administered a neuropsychological battery – a long series of tests specifically aimed at assessing brain functioning, including memory. Sure enough, the tests showed only minimal problems, not nearly enough to account for the frequency with which George pleaded loss of memory.

More important proof came as we were able to stop and catch his specific moments of "memory loss" during our talks.

Eventually, George began to notice that he indeed retreated into this symptom whenever he felt uncomfortable, especially when he felt pressure, angered, or "under the spotlight." He then began to describe a lifetime of avoiding interpersonal strife and pressure by similarly indirect means – adopting a soft spoken and uncompetitive persona, minimizing his ambitiousness, using humor to defuse any tense moment, etc. Finally, and here's the real proof, as we discussed all this his "memory problem" abated. Instead, he began to express his anxieties more directly, in words. He also lost his temper for the first time in years.

George was lost. He was unaware of his anxieties, his interpersonal behavior, his tactics of avoidance, even what symptom he had. Instead, he'd latched onto the idea of a memory problem and used it in service of avoiding confrontation. At uncomfortable moments in session he would plead memory loss, ending the conversation.

I said I would emphasize throughout this book that therapy is a logical, non-mysterious process, so let me start with this case. I did not come up with my ideas about George's true problems by dipping into a secret bag of esoteric and abstruse psychological tenets. They came from very concrete facts. 1) The pattern of George's claim of loss of memory or concentration just at the moment when he, or anyone, might feel at least slightly pressured. 2) My irritation, which I have learned sometimes comes from a feeling that I'm being subtly controlled, especially in contrast with the sympathy I felt on the surface for George and his apparent helplessness. 3) The test results. 4) George's burst of energy, insight, and memories as we began to discuss this possibility that "memory loss" was really a ploy to avoid anxiety. 5) The improvement in George's memory, i.e. the abating of the symptom.

In deciding whether or not psychotherapy is working for you, these last two points are crucial. You should be experiencing symptom relief as well as this kind of epiphany, this "aha! That's what I've been doing/ feeling/thinking; that's who I am". Otherwise, why go?

This notion that facts and logic drive the psychotherapy process goes a long way in countering the flood of abstract, even bizarre hypotheses that can clutter and confuse a person and a therapy session. You may have heard yourself or others wondering such things as "Maybe I sabotage myself", "Maybe I'm afraid of success", "Maybe I resent my wife", "Maybe I don't want to be the boss", "Maybe I'm afraid of commitment", "Maybe I need a vacation", "Maybe I'm the type of person who ...", "Maybe I'm a compulsive, an addict, a depressive, a type A, a type B, a ...." One can only answer, "maybe the sky has turned green while we've been talking"; the only way to know is to back up and look at the facts.

Some of psychotherapy's negative stigma is the product of a very common experience: Put into words, psychotherapy can seem rather obvious. One thinks: Of course Tom's phobia came from feelings about having to ask for money; that's clear as soon as you hear the history. Certainly you could have guessed early on what was up with Bully and Sandra, from chapter 1. Of course your depressed friend has nothing to be depressed about; why can't he see it? Why can't you just tell him so, give him some books about depression and how to overcome it, and end the problem that way? Of course the overly timid, withdrawn, and cautious man became that way from growing up with an intolerant and volatile parent; everyone else who knows the family can see that; and everyone also sees that this man has no reason any longer to be so afraid. Why can't he see it and get moving with his life? Of course the arrogant know-it-all only irritates the very people he's trying to impress; why can't he see that and keep quiet a bit, so that he doesn't end up jobless and friendless?

The short answer is that it's too painful. Although your depressed friend suffers, he is stuck in this depression partly because it is easier to feel depressed and attribute it to one's looks, love life, job, home, whatever, than to face what really hurts, or scares. Meanwhile the rest of us can only drop our jaws in disbelief as this handsome, talented, successful man mopes that he has nothing and is worthless. The bright and attractive woman who attaches herself to one unreliable and dishonest man after another prefers – at an unconscious level – to cry or rage over the current man's behavior rather than to feel and acknowledge some more pervasive and unwieldy problems with herself and her life. Closer to the surface, more consciously, it may feel safer and more familiar to stay in a destructive relationship than to face solitude. That's what we saw with Carl in chapter 1 (yes, men do it too).

Bear in mind that these irrational patterns of feeling, behaving, perceiving are not chosen at a conscious level. Clearly most of us would not engage in such silly and painful habits on purpose. But these habits develop outside of awareness (and nonverbally) where we cannot get at them. This unconsciousness is key to understanding why psychotherapy as opposed to other kinds of help. For just as the problems are established somewhere outside your awareness, so too must the cure reach into that area. Otherwise the treatment won't work.

The more complete answer to these questions – why the patient can't see what is so obvious to us, why books and friends no matter how good sometimes can't help, and why psychotherapy sometimes takes so long compared to other medical or educational programs – is the subject of chapter 5, 6, and the end of chapter 4. There we will see in some detail just what happens in psychotherapy and what obstructs the process.

Finally, let me emphasize that all of the foregoing, as well as the rest of this book, applies to virtually all kinds of patients, not just to intelligent, verbal, and introspective people. The out of control child brought in by desperate parents, even referred by the courts, is lost and stuck in much the same way as were George and Tom in the examples above. His problem is more one of behavior that is disturbing to others rather than feelings and behavior which disturb him, but he is lost just the same. Likewise, his psychotherapy will proceed by much the same steps, even if he refuses to talk for the first five sessions. I have been careful to include case examples in this book that show the whole range of psychotherapy patients and problems. The people I describe are of all ages, economic classes, backgrounds, races, intelligence levels, and they come with all kinds of complaints from the simplest to the most vague and intangible. As we will continue to see, their relief comes from exposing the lies that got them – and keep them – lost and stuck.

CHAPTER 3

A PERSONALITY IS BORN, AND WHY

We begin psychotherapy where psychology itself begins. A patient enters the office with the question: Why do I do what I do, feel what I feel, think what I think, and how can I change it? To answer this question, we have to understand something about personality, where it comes from, how it works. It is personality, after all, that does the doing, feeling, and thinking that are distressing us (or those around us). It is the personality that adopts, or accepts, lies despite what the intellect may know.

Why does the bully bully, the blowhard blow hard, the flincher apologize so relentlessly? Is it a gene? Hardly. Although one's genetic makeup of course has an effect, it does not send a person into psychotherapy. In the realm of personality, genes provide the foundation, and some of the limits. Whether or not that foundation grows into a successful, adaptive, and satisfying personality or into one in distress, depends largely on what happens to that genetic substrate after it is in place. Genes may make someone sensitive and high strung, but it is everything that happens after the genes are in place that decides whether that someone grows into an expressive, open minded, artistic soul, a nail biting, inhibited worrier, an angry, aggressive competitor, or something else.

Remember in chapter 1 we looked at what could happen to a baby who is randomly responded to with frantic, anxious, and frighteningly intense scolding or warning. That child could adapt by becoming a bully, or a flincher, or a control freak, or an insistent know-it-all. These archetypes and the case examples we've seen so far – George, Tom, "Bully", Sandra, Carl – illustrate two important points. First, personality develops in an interpersonal arena. As will become clearer in later chapters, this fact is crucial to comprehending why psychotherapy. Independent as we may like to believe that we are as adults, our sense of security in the world, of self-esteem, of competence, of who we are, all come out of our interactions as a child. Later events have an effect, but none remotely as powerful, long lasting, and indelible as those early relationships (or lack thereof). If this seems hard to swallow right now, bear with me. The case examples throughout the book will hopefully convince you. (Patients, too, sometimes start psychotherapy with a great deal of skepticism about this point.)

Second, personality derives at least in large part from two core needs – to avoid pain and to maximize mastery. The bully flees his old anxiety, the experience of being startled and scared by his mother's sudden outbursts, by adopting a personality that precludes anyone ever hurting or scaring him again. He rushes in with an "I don't care what you think, I do what I want, you can't hurt me, in fact I can hurt you sooner and worse" attitude which gives him at the same time some sense of control and mastery. Granted, his method is not the most productive, but that is the way he develops. The flincher flees the same anxiety more directly. First with his mother, later everywhere, he refrains from asserting himself. When he does speak up, he proceeds timidly, apologizing profusely, preemptively. In this way, he minimizes the chance of experiencing that old frightening and humiliating censure while, like the bully, wresting some control. Battling these same anxieties, the control freak learns and does and knows all, thereby keeping himself as far as possible from the lost, uncertain, bewildered child he once was.

If these three do not develop more flexible and successful ways of keeping their anxiety at bay, they will have problems. Always intimidating others in an effort to quiet his own anxieties, the bully could end up friendless, jobless, physically hurt if he bullies the wrong person, and alone. The flincher may drive everyone away with his constant apologizing and need for reassurance. Or people may simply drop out of his life; he is so withdrawn and bland that they forget about him. Loneliness and ambition may torment him, but he will be too timid to do anything about them. The control freak puts everyone off with his relentless expertise; he might even be fired for it, or for professing expertise where in fact he has none. He may eventually be unable to function because the need to control overwhelms his judgment about what is worth controlling, or what is possible to control.

These people are caught up in old tactics that not only don't work anymore but work against them. Tactics which were originally developed to provide a sense of safety and control now cause loss of jobs, friends, colleagues, intimacy, in short all the things that really do give us some safety, happiness, and control. Understanding the specifics of how a person is trying, however misguidedly, to minimize pain and maximize mastery is central to psychotherapy. However painful the symptoms are, they were developed as defenses, in response to basic needs. Not surprisingly, therefore, people do not easily let go of them. Try asking a control freak to "lighten up" sometime.

The depressed person is a good example of this dynamic. Most of us have met people who seem resolutely, irrationally, and pointlessly pessimistic. Resolutely because there seems to be no altering their point of view; irrationally, because no data to the contrary seems to matter to that point of view; and pointlessly of course because such an outlook only ruins their chances for any kind of success or happiness. So why do they stick to it?

Often we find in such patients that in childhood there were experiences of rejection, abandonment, profound loneliness. Again, remember that such experiences are uncomfortable to an adult but literally life-threatening to a child; without the most basic of attention from the adults around him, a child can die. At the emotional level, the effects are no less devastating. A child's personality develops in large part from the responses he gets to his actions. Watch a child pick up something for the first time. Watch as he then looks eagerly around for his parent's response. From this interaction, he learns a basic sense of his own power and value. Without it, he has to struggle with isolation, humiliation, abandonment, and his basic helplessness as a child. If this sounds extreme, think honestly how you felt the last time you tried to tell something exciting to someone close to you and were ignored. Now multiply that feeling by about a thousand to get a sense of what the experience is like for a child. It is, in fact, intolerable to him; he must find some alternative to the abandonment.

A common way for a child to do this is to believe that there is something wrong with him and with what he has done. This is what we saw in Fred, Sandra, and Carl in chapter 1; the boy's epiphany at the end of *Good Will Hunting* was that he blames himself for the abuse. This erroneous belief – this lie – protects the child from the more unwieldy and despairing reality that he is alone. It allows him hope, the possibility that if he can just identify and change what is so wrong with him he will then have a home, safety, connection. Incidentally, can you hear the fantasy of control in this distorted point of view, that there is some way to stop the abandonment? The adult depressive's point of view is among other things a remnant of the child's "there is something wrong with me". Some depressed people believe "maybe if I can figure it out (or lose weight, jog faster, earn more, score with the babes...), I won't be so miserable"; such people often display a lot of anxiety and worrying, what we used to call "agitated depression". (Please note that not all depressives suffer from these exact dynamics and that even in those who do, there other aspects to their depression. I am describing what I have found to be a central component in many depressed people; it is not the whole story.)

You may notice in the case examples so far – Carl in particular – the beginning of an answer to my original title for this book, "Why Psychotherapy". Why can't Carl, the depressed person, the bully, the flincher simply see the errors of their ways and change. In briefest terms, as we saw with Carl, the answer is this: Painful as they are, those ways began as protection against even more horrific experiences. Better to be a loser who is trying to improve than to be isolated, abandoned, and powerless to fix it. At least a loser had a home, if only he could figure out how to belong there.

Minimizing pain and maximizing mastery are basic to personality because they are basic to life. Consider what happens to a human being over the course of a life. Initially, you live in a warm, virtually stress-free womb, perfectly suited to your needs. You don't have to eat; food goes directly into your bloodstream via the umbilical cord, already digested and processed. You don't have to move. You don't have to ask for anything, wait for anything, wear anything – the environment is constantly same temperature as your body. You don't even have to breathe.

Then suddenly you are thrust into the world. (Remember the newborn baby in the movie *Look Who's Talking* screaming in Bruce Willis' voice "Oh, no! Put me back! It's cold!") You can't breathe but you have to; to that end a huge and strange creature wearing a mask slaps you on the rump. Now the limits start. You can't just eat when you want to; first you have to get attention, which is hard because you haven't learned to talk yet. If anything else is bothering you, your parents have to figure it out without your help, and you have to wait around until they do.

More frustrations follow. Soon your parents insist on leaving you alone all night, you can't defecate when and where you want, and you have to start wearing clothes. Then you have to put them on yourself. Then you have to eat foods you don't like. Then you have to stop hitting your sibling every time you're frustrated. Then you have chores. Eventually you have to leave the house and obey a whole other system of rules and requirements. Ultimately, you have to become self-sufficient, handling all of life's complexities on your own. Just when you get used to that, your body starts to deteriorate requiring more care and accommodation. If life is such a trial why not just hide under the bed? Why doesn't the traumatized child whose mother overreacted when he tried to touch something in the house simply retreat into inaction?

The reason that doesn't happen is because for about 3 billion years, life on this planet has survived precisely because of its prowess and aggressiveness in not only avoiding pain and danger, but also searching out and conquering – mastering – the world around it. When the first one-celled creatures floating in the ocean began wrapping themselves around food particles and ingesting them to provide fuel for reproduction, the ego was born. The ego is that part of us that seeks to explore and master the environment; it seeks to attain from the world the maximum food, resources, money, dominance, power, pleasure that it can. And the purpose of all this activity has not changed since the first one-celled ocean dweller: To maximize the chance for survival and procreation. For 3 billion years the creatures who were best at this activity were the ones who survived against predators and the elements. They were the ones who best survived the cold, the heat, the ebbs in food supply. They were also, once sexual reproduction became part of the picture, the best at attracting a mate.

So by the time humans came around – 30 thousand to 4.5 million years ago, depending on what you call "human" – the child reaching for objects in his house was acting out a 3 billion year old habit, an instinct bred into every cell in his body. If such a child is scolded for it, he still has to find outlets for those instincts.

The interplay of these aspects of the personality – reaching out to master and retreating back to safety – is in large part what defines our functioning. Reaching out to touch something, including a hot stove top, is an act of the ego, the self. Learning not to touch objects that are hot, or to test them first, is the ego's adaptation to the environment in order to minimize pain and danger. The balance of the two is an ever-shifting dance of feelings and needs that follows us throughout life. You can see it in the child's struggle to jump off a high diving board despite his fears, in the adult's indecision over opening his own business or staying with the old firm, in the struggle at any age to go strike up a conversation and risk rejection or stay put where it's safe. And of course, we saw it in Bully's changing modes of finding power and dominance. As the schoolyard bully, the high school achiever, the young businessman, and even the phobic 30 something, he was working to avoid the agony of his early victim role and at the same time to reach out for sustenance and power in the world.

How we navigate this dance, how we adapt to frustration and anxiety while seeking to master what we can, defines who we are, our personality. It is formed out of our genetic makeup combined with our early experiences and relationships. Personality elaborates and becomes ever more unique, as we saw in Bully, but the core remains and defines us forever.

Exploring this core, even if briefly, is part of most successful psychotherapy. In such exploration, we finally make sense of what has been so perplexing and disturbing in our behavior and feelings. It brings those moments of realization that patients experience in a productive session, moments that lead to real and blessed change – change in outlook, behavior, feelings, which is of course the goal of therapy. Further case examples later in this book will illustrate this process.

In this chapter I have tried to sketch out why a personality is born, why you have one. I tried to show how two main, primitive goals of our existence may lead to much of our later irrational and perplexing feelings and behavior. In the next chapter we will trace in more detail how the initial tactics – and earliest lies – of the bully, the flincher, the control freak, and others develop into the irrational and counterproductive feelings and behavior that we call "symptoms".

CHAPTER 4

DEFENSES AND SYMPTOMS

Let's reiterate three main points: 1) People seek psychological treatment when they are lost or stuck; 2) symptoms are the expression of being lost or stuck; 3) symptoms arise out of core features of our personalities. Now why should these be? Why should Tom's anxieties, anger, and humiliation, which arise when he has to ask for money, be turned into an elevator phobia? Why should symptoms come when one has lost one's way, lost track of one's feelings and experiences, and why lose track of those things in the first place? Why believe the lies – the ones we tell ourselves or the ones we were told – when the data tell us not to? The answer lies in understanding symptoms and defenses.

We all have an intuitive sense at least of what a defense is. We recognize it in the behaviors of the bully, the flincher, and the control freak from the previous chapter. When we tell little Suzie to pick up the toy she has discarded she erupts with "I didn't put it there!", when Jim treats Jenny with extra coldness and disinterest while we all know he's sweet on her, we speak of these behaviors as "defensive." What we mean is that the person is trying, in an especially obvious and graceless manner, to avoid the pain and to maximize mastery of their uncomfortable spot – to maintain control of and invulnerability to the interpersonal situation. Suzie is feeling accused, put down, even humiliated; Jim, too, feels – or anticipates feeling – humiliated, unattractive, rejected. Rather than acknowledge these unpleasant experiences, they devote their energy to defense, to protecting themselves.

Now imagine Jim was an especially sensitive kid, so threatened by this kind of rejection that he grew up extra vigilant, anticipating it in all situations. In response, he redoubles his bravado, behaving towards others with ever more disinterest, independence, "cool". Later he starts treating his wife this way, his clients, his boss and coworkers. Now suppose he loses his job and must interview for a new one. With this added pressure of potential humiliation and rejection, he becomes even more off-putting in his feigned indifference. Needless to say, no-one will hire him. At this point, someone – maybe a last remaining and trusted friend – gets him to consider that fact that his job interviews are failing despite his excellent credentials, that he hasn't made a friend in years, and that he seems hopelessly uptight. What began with Jim being a "defensive" child has bloomed into a personality checkered with symptoms: anxiety, occupational and social failures, probably a troubled marriage at this point, and an attitude that gets him labeled as someone with "personality problems".

In Jim we see how a symptom is an outgrowth of a defense. Defenses protect us from rejection, dismissal, abandonment, accusation, and other assaults to our self-esteem. When these defenses fail to <u>contain</u> those experiences – to shield us from the pain of them – we usually escalate our efforts. At that point, behaviors tend to emerge that we or those around us find perplexing, distressing, counterproductive, irrational. That behavior is labeled a symptom. We might usefully think of symptoms as defenses run amok.

Take a look again at the case of "Bully" from chapter 1. He came to treatment complaining of marital discord and anxiety symptoms, but prior to the emergence of these problems he was obsessive, perfectionistic, impatient, and depressed. The degree to which the first three of these are upsetting to him and/or to others, how disruptive they are to the pursuit of his goals and pleasures, determines in large part whether we call them "personality traits" or "symptoms". As the latter, we then suspect the presence of a "disorder" such as Panic Disorder, Depressive Disorder, Persistent Depressive Disorder (Dysthymia) otherwise known as mild depression, Generalized Anxiety Disorder, Agoraphobia, Unspecified Obsessive-Compulsive and Related Disorder (it's really called that), and so on.

Remember the flincher who had the same childhood experiences as the bully? He grows up to be relentlessly apologetic and timid. In him, the original physical flinching has been internalized into interpersonal moments, an inner clenching/tightening. He avoids situations that might bring about that flinching. He lives alone, rarely disagrees, rarely dates; his stomach lurches (flinches) when he has to meet new people, he breaks out in rashes at parties, and his hobbies are largely solitary. At this point, his behavior fits into a defense pattern we might characterize as Avoidant. Meanwhile the rashes and stomach butterflies qualify as anxiety symptoms.

Imagine that as the years go by the flincher begins to suffer greater loneliness, not an unlikely scenario. He is therefore motivated to seek out more social contact, but this brings on more of his anxieties, more flinching. Here he might present himself to a therapist with social phobias, fear of public speaking/humiliation, or even angry disgust with other people's failure to give him more attention and support. If he does not get help with these problems, he could well remain ever more acutely trapped by his competing agendas of wanting a social life and being made intensely anxious when seeking one out.

Ultimately, he may become listless, hopeless. The loneliness and anxiety mount to the point that even routine daily activities become too burdensome and he can hardly find the motivation to do anything. His home and appearance begin to deteriorate. He is now exhibiting symptoms which might get him diagnosed with a depressive disorder or even Schizoid Personality Disorder. What began as a defensive reaction – flinching – developed into a lifestyle organized around avoiding anxiety; this defense then failed, leaving him with symptoms of depression or a personality disorder.

Don't forget that all of this happens unconsciously. These people – the bully, the flincher, Tom, the control freak – do not know what is bothering them, only that they are increasingly bothered. If they knew – really knew, remembered in full – what was upsetting them, they would not need to behave as they do. So the bully must either remember the long buried humiliation or continue bullying in his effort to flee that experience. The flincher must remember it so that he can stop fearing it everywhere, so that he can attach all that anxiety to the past where it was warranted and where it originated. By doing this, he will be freed from its inhibiting effects on his life and able to move from just avoiding anxiety to more substantial and gratifying goals.

Defensive behavior comes in two main forms. We do what we had to in order to survive, and we do what was done to us; the flincher adopted the former defense, the bully the latter. This fact is best known to all of us who have gotten into long term relationships, especially if we've had children. What do we all find to our horror? That we say and do the exact same insufferable things our parents did. (Obviously, this is not always a defense. Sometimes it's the best course of action. Our parents weren't always wrong.) But when the behavior we exhibit is counterproductive, irrational, contrary to our best interest and not what we would choose yet emerges automatically then we are in the throes of a defensive reaction.

Symptoms emerge or become more pronounced when the defense fails to protect us from what we unconsciously believe to be intolerable anxiety and pain. Sometimes symptoms are exaggerations of original defensive adaptations. Bully's irritation and tendency towards violence were exaggerations of his original defensive reaction of doing what was done to him, a pushing away any hint of anxiety and weakness; he also bullied as a kind of displaced rage at being made to feel so scared and inadequate. Sometimes symptoms are the avoided emotions and experiences themselves, leaking out through other defenses, as in Bully's panic and phobias. Usually both kinds of symptoms coexist.

I have been describing symptoms and defenses up to this point using very simple examples. In the real world things are more complex. Bully's anxiety symptoms are more than his old fears leaking out; they are themselves defensive, despite their seeming to be unrelated to his basic defense of bullying, of pushing away and denying his weaknesses.

Just like his bullying, they are protecting him from the same experiences he has always defended against – fright and humiliation as a child. They are lies, distractions from his real anxieties. Do we really believe he panics over an elevator? Or that mild disagreement from his wife is reasonable explanation for this otherwise rational man to become violent? Or that the merest inadequacy from a new employee could really send him into such rage that he has to struggle against the impulse to fire the man on the spot? No, and in his clearer moments, Bully doesn't either. His true anxieties come from a time when his life really was that threatening and enraging, when his emotional and even physical survival were truly in danger.

Symptoms have been described as <u>compromises</u> in some of the early writings in psychoanalysis, and we can see this in Bully. His anxiety symptoms give vent to some of the original and terrifying emotion, but in the relatively safer context of his present day life. The feelings have to come out somehow, but he cannot tolerate their full weight as they originally happened; instead, he attaches them to more innocuous stimuli, just as the flincher habitually does. It is easier for Bully to experience a phobia than the very real and at the time life threatening rage of his father. Symptoms protect us from remembering incapacitating emotions in their original context; at the same time they provide enough of an outlet for all that emotion so that we can continue to meet the demands of his daily life. In this way, then, Bully's anxiety symptoms are both 1) the leaking out of his original fears <u>and</u> 2) a defense, a means of <u>avoiding</u> those original fears.

Here is a more extended case example illustrating symptoms and defenses. Ron came to see me complaining of indecision and obsessing ("thinking too much") which had virtually immobilized him, fear of losing his job, a troubled relationship, and pervasive high anxiety. He described many months of unhappiness with his girlfriend, yet felt unable to make a decision about her. He worked at a high level in the corporate world and was quite successful and respected in his field, but his work was being hampered by indecision. He obsessed over decisions he was more than competent and experienced enough to make quickly, and he was experiencing an ever increasing feeling of inadequacy which he feared was always about to be discovered as justified.

As we talked a striking phenomenon emerged. Despite Ron's high intelligence, education, and verbal skills, it often seemed that as soon we were getting somewhere, we would both become confused. As we discussed this, he came upon the image of "the one-way fog", from which he could see out but no-one could see in. It certainly was working on me. In graduate school his classmates had commented on his method of staying safely distant from them; he was described as a charming and fun guy to have around, and yet people complained that they knew nothing about him and could feel no real friendship with him. Once this topic emerged in our sessions, Ron elaborated on this loneliness. He felt it in intimate relationships, in his continued lack of close friends, and in his very strong sense of isolation – again, all of this in spite of his great popularity and the respect he commanded.

How can Ron understand these symptoms, and more important what can he do about them? First, he must understand their function in his life, how they minimize pain and maximize mastery. Although Ron's feelings, worries, and behavior seem irrational from the outside, they are somehow serving that inner agenda. When we understand how, his symptoms will make sense; when Ron understands it (emotionally, in the gut) – when he catches the lies – his misery and symptoms will ease.

Ron's father was an extremely abusive man, taking almost sadistic pleasure in wielding power. Ron described the look of glib satisfaction on his father's face when he told Ron to "Go get the paddle" with which he'd beat Ron. What's more, his father was unpredictable. Ron rarely felt he could anticipate his father's reactions or navigate his moods. In addition to this kind of abuse, Ron told me horrendous stories of abandonment. His parents would take him shopping in a huge mall, and then as punishment for some slight misbehavior they would drive off without him, leaving him alone and scared in the huge parking lot; this at age five. They would return later and laugh at Ron's distress. His father also warned him not to cry, under threat of further physical punishment.

So what did Ron do to survive? Until about age six, Ron was hyperactive and a bully. He was doing what was done to him. He also stayed away from home as much as possible, exploring the neighborhood and generally getting himself into trouble. During these years, Ron was being a chip off the old block – aggressive, loud, domineering, active.

Then there was a change. Ron vividly recalls being in the middle of a fight, winning as usual, and suddenly realizing he wasn't even angry at his opponent. He stopped the fight and never went back to such behavior. He became quite the academic achiever, winning state spelling competitions, receiving honors in all his classes, and attending a prestigious college. He even learned to keep out of his father's way, although with only partial success. Ron did not, however, feel much peace with himself, and he was quite isolated. He always found he was staying safely behind the "one-way fog", unable to loosen up and join in the fun (although from the outside, others often thought he was).

Remember again that all of this was unconscious. When we began working together Ron knew only that in those days he was <u>seen as</u> secretive and removed; he did not really remember being that way and was only vaguely aware of feeling chronically lonely. It was only when this process of fogging emerged between him and me during sessions that he remembered all the comments he'd heard over the years about his opacity, and began to remember how he felt all that time.

Ron had moved from an early and rather obvious defensive style of doing what was done to him to a more intellectually driven one – a kind of stop-and-think. Although a much more successful defense, it held the seeds of the anxiety symptoms and obsessing that eventually brought him to see me: Early on he was overly cautious, slow to make simple decisions, obsessive and driven in his academic work. Despite his popularity he was isolated. He was careful to present a well practiced and sunny disposition, entertaining and personable, as he had done to survive with his volatile father. Still, his defenses at this point worked at least superficially. They brought him academic success, a superficial popularity, and some meager protection from his father's displeasure. They were what he learned to do in order to survive.

But this rather tenuous adjustment did not last. By the time Ron came to see me his defenses were failing him. He was relying on them in a rigid, unproductive, even destructive, way. He was so obsessing over whether and how to break up with his current girlfriend that he was immobile. The relationship had been unsatisfying and quite frankly a mess for over six of the nine months they'd been together, yet he would mentally rehash the same pros and cons, the same scenarios, the same memories, over and over, all the while taking no action. The same phenomenon was interfering with his job performance. In general, he complained, he was "wired and uptight all the time and I don't see why". The same stop-and-think defense that had originally saved him from a life of bullying, that had bought him academic and social success, had now run amok and was making him miserable.

At the same time, intrusive and distressing as the obsessing was, it was protecting him, as is the role of any defense. It was providing a sense of control and mastery, a feeling that he had everything clear and sorted out and under good control – or at least that he was working towards such meticulous understanding. This feeling of control was ever more necessary as his anxiety level rose, faced as he was with deciding about his girlfriend and probably losing the relationship. You may recognize similarities here with Carl from chapter 1.

Also like Carl, obsessing in this way protected Ron not just from anxiety but from rage. That little boy who was so randomly terrorized by his father was – is – furious; that's partly why he was such a thug himself when he was very young. Rage in obsessive people is very often among the most buried of material, the hardest to bring to the surface. When it remains buried therapy usually stalls. This is partly the reason why the therapist in *Ordinary People,* discussed in chapter 1, needles the boy so much.

To return now to the security function of his defenses, Ron felt such security was necessary for him to function at his job. Meetings were causing ever increasing anxiety, almost to the point of panic. Obsessing helped him feel just secure enough to face the clients who looked to him for solutions to their companies' problems. Most of all, the obsessing protected him by preventing his taking any real action. He did not have to actually face a decision about his girlfriend, or anything else, because he would become immobilized in a quagmire of endless reconsideration. He did not have to risk making a wrong decision and the endless weighing of pros and cons also blocked any awareness of rage.

Of course, this protection was very unsatisfying or he would not have come to see me. It left him trapped in a miserable relationship, allowed him no pleasure or ease in his work, increased his need for distance from others, and in general kept him "wired and uptight all the time". So why did he cling to this obsessing?

The question cannot be answered by looking into Ron's current life. His obsessing was not based in the present. Ron had no real reason to fear anything about his job; remember he was competent, successful, and respected, and he loved his work. His girlfriend was, as he later put it, a "nondecision". The relationship was over half a year before he sought help; they just hadn't actually broken up. As for the fear of being alone, Ron was never particularly close to this girlfriend to begin with and he was quite adept at meeting and wooing women. There would be no shortage of companionship when he wanted it. So again why such trouble making the move? What was all the fuss?

When there is nothing in the present circumstances to account for the symptoms, then the answer lies somewhere else. Ron did not really fear displeasing his girlfriend or being alone or being fired from his job or anything else in his current life; he had no reason to be obsessing about any of that. Those were distractions – lies. What he feared was his father. The current stressors were triggers of that old anxiety. As the anxiety rose, as his better coping mechanisms failed him, Ron fell back on the same defensive operation – stop and think – that originally enabled him to move beyond a life of random bullying, of doing what was done to him.

This was an unconscious dynamic as all defenses are. When Ron came in, he knew that something was exaggerated in his stop-and-think habit, and in his reactions to current life, but those reactions still felt very real to him. He did believe, at least sometimes, that his girlfriend and job were the sources of his problems. In this, Ron is similar to the elevator phobic who can't shake the belief that the elevator really is the source of his anxiety, even though having read all the statistics this phobic person knows better than the rest of us just how safe elevators really are.

The "one-way fog", too, becomes a logical behavior when viewed as an old habit, as a reaction to his father rather than to anything in the present. This symptom served as a compromise between the conflicting demands of desiring social contact and the dangers of interaction – danger of his father in a largely unconscious past, despite Ron's superficial memory of the raw facts of his childhood. The "fog" allowed Ron contact with others while affording him "the safety of not being seen", as he once put it. For in his childhood it was only by not being seen that he was safe from his father's violence. From behind the fog, Ron could carefully read his father's moods, a necessary survival skill in his house. This pattern of retreating to a safe observation point emerged everywhere in his life – at work, with friends, at social gatherings, and in session with me. The more he liked someone and the more he desired real contact with them, the more he withdrew into the fog.

This is a good time to emphasize again that psychotherapy is a logical, accessible process, not faith healing. I don't assert that Ron was suffering from past angst because that's what Freud or someone else said; I say it because all the data point that way. 1) Ron's anxiety symptoms were not limited to one or two areas of his life. If he had a worry about his girlfriend's instability, for example, why would he be immobile, indecisive, and miserable in so many other areas of his life? 2) There are no data even suggesting a basis in present day reality for his anxiety and helplessness. In fact, everything he and I knew about his life showed that his feelings were completely irrational as reactions to anything in the present. No one was threatening him with anything, he was very popular and respected, and he was nothing but competent. 3) In trying to account for his unhappiness and anxiety, the only thing that begins to explain the intensity of the feelings is his experience with his father.

And last: When Ron began to make the connection between his current discomfort and the experiences of his childhood – when he stopped lying to himself that "I know what happened" and instead allowed himself to re-experience it, to feel it – there was change. His symptoms cleared up, his mood improved drastically, and he experienced a flood of new insight about himself and his life. These reactions are always the final proof that we have hit the right material in psychotherapy. The change in mood and perspective is key in judging whether or not you are getting anything out of the treatment.

I cannot emphasize that last phenomenon strongly enough. If it never happens, what is the point in going to treatment? It is in fact the most important piece of data you have in judging whether psychotherapy is helping you. If you can't feel the change Ron did at least once in a while, then you have no reason to accept your psychologist's contention that your real problem is not the phobia, girlfriend, boyfriend, mother, drug, or obsession that you think it is, but rather is something you may hardly have considered.

Here is an example from a bit later in Ron's treatment that demonstrates this moment of insight. He eventually developed a rather solid relationship with a new girlfriend. He found he was telling her things about himself he'd never told anyone except me. He was openly discussing his treatment, his anxieties, his struggles with his "demons". This was quite a change from his previous retreat behind the one-way fog.

He was happier with her than he'd been with anyone and he felt better than he could ever remember feeling. Work was engaging and felt "like a dance". But one day he came in and asked me why he felt so driven, just as this relationship was becoming so rewarding, to go out and sleep with every woman he could get his hands on.

He said, "I think I want to push her away", and suggested that he was afraid of being hurt by this woman. This bit of self-analysis may sound logical on the surface, but there are holes in the reasoning. Mainly, he really was smitten and there was simply no data suggesting that she was either pressuring him to move the relationship forward faster or that she was about to leave him. Ron could find no hint of a dark side in all the months they had been together.

But I didn't have to go into any of that with Ron, nor did I mention the many other reasons why his speculation did not seem plausible to me. Instead I asked him, "Does that [analysis of his behavior] ring true?" He thought for a moment and decided it did not. I then asked him to think about exactly what he feared in being close to this girlfriend – feared in fantasy, because in reality there was of course little to fear; she was not in reality about to leave him or "turn psycho" (his term). He thought a moment and then said, with a new energy and sorrow in his voice and face, "abandoned, desolate, empty, having nothing, and I'll close up forever". I asked did this statement ring, and his answer was a resounding "Yes! Big time; I can feel that." He then went on to elaborate on the "knot of anxiety" in his gut that he always felt when he thought about this woman, and how the knot would send him into a frenzy of girl chasing, something he didn't even particularly enjoy anymore. He remembered moments of similar anxiety from other times in his life, and again he realized there was a deep sense of horrific loneliness that he was fleeing. These thoughts resonated with Ron; they "clicked"; they felt right to him, like accurate descriptions of his inner life, his <u>experience</u>, his self. This is data one can never argue with. Compare it with his tepid reaction when I asked if his original hypothesizing resonated in this way. So he wasn't afraid of this woman leaving him; he was afraid of an old experience of much more profound isolation and helplessness, such as when he was left in those parking lots by his parents.

At those times in his childhood Ron really was "abandoned, desolate, empty, having nothing". It seems very reasonable – logical – that the fear of repeating that horrible experience surfaces when, after all the years of "one-way fog", he finally becomes intimate with someone. In light of dreading that awful desolation and fear from childhood, a little mania and compulsivity even to the point of ruining a nice relationship begin to seem less irrational.

Notice that on the surface Ron's original statement about why he might be feeling driven to chase other women is not much different from what he eventually discovered – that he feared abandonment. But there is a crucial difference between his first statement and his later ones. The first statement was Ron's speculation, his guess, unconnected from any emotional resonance and from any truth about his life. It was a "Maybe" statement of the kind I described towards the end of chapter 2. As such, it had no impact. Again, any interpretation in a therapy session, whether it comes from you or from the therapist, is useful only if it has inner resonance, if it makes you feel an "aha! There I am!" If it does not in this way ring true for you, it is unlikely to open your eyes, expose any lies, and free you from symptoms. It may be an interesting possibility, but it will remain just that – academic, intellectual, devoid of any power to heal.

By contrast, we know that Ron's subsequent exploration of his feelings and behavior was on the right track from his strong reaction to that exploration. First, he showed heightened emotion and excited recognition. Then came a flood of thoughts, feelings, and memories. He recalled past incidents dating back to childhood in which he felt similarly desolate, empty, and isolated, similarly desperate for but hopeless to obtain comfort and reassurance. He immediately saw how constant such feelings were in his life, how they affected his friendships, his relationships at work, our interactions in session, and more. He saw that he kept everyone at a distance out of fear that he would be left high and dry, awash in the old agonizing helplessness and isolation, just he actually was left by his family.

Of course the final proof that Ron was on the right track was the subsequent change of behavior and attitude. Over the ensuing weeks and months, Ron no longer needed to frantically chase women and he began to enjoy the relationship with his girlfriend. He was much more relaxed with friends, with me, and in his job. His performance evaluations at work reflected this change. His superiors no longer reported his being "distant and insufficiently engaged".

Before ending this chapter, we should briefly discuss just what I mean by "data", a word I've been using a lot here. Data in psychotherapy are feelings, behavior, thoughts, perceptions, and external facts, yours and mine. But be clear: If you tell me you are lonely, the data are not that you are lonely; the data are that you <u>said</u> you are lonely. Meanwhile my perception may be that you are behaving more like a person who is angry than one who is lonely, and my perception is also a piece of data. In our session together, we will have to reconcile these seemingly disparate perceptions. It may be that you are mistaken about what you feel. It may be that you do feel lonely but are also angry. It may be that you are tense and wary of criticism when you talk to me, which I misinterpret as anger. There are many possibilities. When we find the right answer, you will have learned something about who you are. You will have become a little less lost. But until we hit the right answer, most of what we talk about will be speculation, like Ron's first guesses about why he wanted to push his girlfriend away. It can be a necessary step but such speculation doesn't go far unless you check in with you inner response to each possibility. This step can be missed in highly intelligent, verbal folk who enjoy reasoning things out – itself a defense, as we saw in Ron and as we'll discuss in later chapters.

Consider another example of what is and isn't data. If you tell me in a manner that I perceive as smug, superior, and impatient that you cannot come to the next session, there are several pieces of data to explore.

First, is it true that you cannot come or are you reluctant to schedule things so that you can? Second, we have to deal with my perception that you were smug, superior, and impatient. I may hypersensitive, I may be misreading things, I may be unaware of my own irritation or hurt feelings, or you may have been as nasty as I perceived. To resolve the matter, we must appeal to other data: Do I usually perceive such things in people? Is it my tendency to be hypersensitive? Are you often accused of being nasty? Is it my tendency to drive people to speak thus to me? Is it habitual for you to vent like that and to then deny it? Is this really how you speak all the time and if so, has no one ever pointed it out to you? Is there any reason for me to be hypersensitive and hurt in the current situation? Is there any reason for you to be angry at me today? Perhaps – more data – we will find that you had to rush from work to get to my office today; then after all that effort I was running late, leaving you to fume in the waiting room. But this conflicts with your politeness, your awareness that it is not unusual for me to be 5 or even 10 minutes late (and I always make up the time), your desire to preserve our good rapport. Perhaps we'll find out that you're sick of other people's demands on you and for whatever reason you suddenly decided to assert yourself in the context of our relationship instead of to your boss, husband, wife, business partner, or your teenaged daughter. As with the couple, "A" and "B" who I mentioned in chapter 1, this is a lot of potential cans of worms to sort through! How much simpler to skip over all that's happening, to just lie about it.

If you say, "Maybe I really don't want to marry that person", or "maybe I'd feel better in a different job", now you are speculating and even farther from the data. That is what Ron was doing when he said "I think I want to push [my girlfriend] away". If you say, "I think I was anxious," don't stop there. Ask yourself if you _felt_ anxious? Did you behave in a manner we recognize as anxious? Did others say you were behaving in such a way? Can we find a plausible reason for your being anxious – taking into account all we know (more data) about what does and does not scare you?

This kind of exploration can feel exhausting especially if you're really trying to avoid the topic – we'll talk more about that in the next chapter on resistance – but it is necessary in psychotherapy. It brings the moments of learning that leave patients feeling clearer, calmer, stronger, more centered, more powerful, and as one patient put it "just plain saner". It is a pattern you can see within a single session and also over time as treatment progresses.

When you make contact with what you are genuinely experiencing inside, when you stop lying to yourself, you feel better and function better. This is the one piece of magic psychotherapy offers.

In this chapter, we have sketched how early interpersonal relationships give rise to defenses and symptoms, to personality dynamics. These dynamics follow us as a constant throughout our lives, despite what may appear on the outside to be vast changes. Ron and "Bully" changed during their lives yet remained rooted in their core dynamics, continually battling against and at the same time reenacting their pasts. Those original dynamics were at the bottom of the problems that finally brought them into psychotherapy, although they traveled a long route before showing up at my door complaining of phobias, obsessing, indecision, immobility, panic attacks, anxiety, angry outbursts, and marital problems.

Now the question becomes what to do about symptoms and defenses. It may sound from the case examples given so far that the cure is simple: Remember thy pain and ye shall be set free. True, but the process is never this direct. If it were, we could simply listen to our friends, therapists, or self-help books, try out new behaviors, watch them work, and wrap the whole thing up in a month.

That scenario ignores how and why the problem behaviors and feelings originated. Don't forget that symptoms and defenses are rooted in experiences which formed the core of our personalities. You can't just cut them out like tumors. They are formed at a largely unconscious level and devoted to keeping out of awareness the core issues that we need to uncover. So you can't expect to "just get over it". Your defenses are going to conspire against you even seeing the "it" you need to get over. We saw that in Ron and Carl and Sandra, who obsessed over a concrete distraction rather than notice what was really happening to them, and we saw it in chapter 1 with Fred and Karen simply editing out of memory not only what they felt but what they said and did. Exactly how defenses and symptoms remain so stubbornly unconscious and so resistant to change – and how psychotherapy breaks through that resistance and frees people to change – are the subjects of the next chapter. There we will begin to see "why psychotherapy".

CHAPTER 5

EXPOSING LIES: RESISTANCE AND THE PROCESS OF PSYCHOTHERAPY

I once heard a radio psychologist talking about perplexing and self-destructive behaviors. He pointed out that we engage in these – particularly in our relationships – because we have internalized and continue to act out early relationships with our parents. He went on to say that we must actively explore how in our current painful situations, whatever they are, we are seeking out people and things to stand in for our mother and/or father; he stated that when we see of such patterns in our lives, we will no longer need to act them out, to repeat them.

This kind of thing goes way back. Freud called it "transference" and talked in much more depth about it. This more superficial version is common in the self-help and popular psychology literature, and it sounds like what I have said so far about how psychotherapy works. There is, however, an important difference. I am saying – and this is supported by research as well as by Freud – that it is the <u>emotional experience</u> that is crucial to recall, not the intellectual details of the parallels between early parental relationships and current feelings and behavior, however interesting or even compelling those details are. Without recall of that emotional experience, such parallels are just interesting stories with no real power to bring about change. Ron, in the previous chapter, needed to become conscious of – to remember and feel – the intensity of his abandonment fears; the fact that those fears center on real events from his time living with his father and mother is secondary. The moment of healing came when he made contact with feeling "abandoned, desolate, empty", not during his prior speculations about "pushing [his girlfriend] away" nor even afterward when he recalled other times in his life of similar emptiness. It was the emotional memory that freed him from using compulsive womanizing to flee horrific memories of abandonment. Obviously, such issues do go way back and most likely began with one or both of his parents; we know that he was subjected to quite traumatic abandonments at an early age, and where else could such persistent and irrational fears be coming from? But again that detail is secondary. The relief came in making contact with the emotion, not with tracing it back to childhood or to anything else. (We saw the same distinction between healing insight and mere intellectual content in Sandra and Bully, in chapter 1.)

This difference between what I am saying here and what the radio psychologist said gets to the heart of a very common, insidious, and destructive problem in talking about psychotherapy. Put into words, psychological concepts and especially the discoveries a patient makes during a session sometimes sound hopelessly obvious and trite. For someone unfamiliar with the process it is easy to think either that the emerging connections are just intellectual constructs of questionable validity or that they are hopelessly obvious? Why, such a person might reasonably ask, should the discoveries take so long? And who needs an expert for such simple ideas? Why can't one just read about them?

The answer lies in the difference described above. With Ron – as with Sandra, and "Bully", and others we will discuss – the key element was <u>not</u> making a connection between the present and the past; that was secondary. The primary curative ingredient of our session was his making contact with the <u>experience</u> he was having – the panic about his independence and about being abandoned. It is the <u>feeling</u> that needs to be brought into consciousness, the pain that is being avoided by the acting out, by the symptoms; it is less important to trace where those feelings originated. I cannot state this too strongly, so I encourage you to quickly reread this paragraph.

Of course, one rarely accomplishes the first without the second: Becoming conscious of the pain and remembering one's childhood tend to go hand in hand. The bully needs to become conscious of his fears of humiliation and powerlessness – in doing so, he will probably remember such experiences with his mother or whoever caused them. The flincher, too, needs to remember that same original experience so he can stop fearing it around every corner. But it is awareness of the emotion that releases them from the need to constantly compensate for or avoid those awful experiences, not the knowledge of the connection between current behavior and past pain; memories of childhood will not help without remembering the emotion, the experience of it all, it won't help getting you un-lost and un-stuck, and the mere content won't be very impressive. That is why when psychotherapy is presented in fiction or on talk shows it can sound so trivial, obvious, and flaccid.

To be more specific, let's define experience as a set of feelings and perceptions surrounding an event. Perceptions include the physical, sensual, primitive feel of a thing as much as the conscious ideas and words assigned to it. Bringing an experience into consciousness is thus a different process than making an intellectual connection between the present and the past; bringing an experience into consciousness is physical, sensual, emotional, primitive, and often defies words. By contrast the process of making the intellectual connection is essentially solving an intellectual puzzle, and it is about as useful. It may be fun, you may even get some satisfaction, but it changes little.

Making contact with experiences, whether in the present or in memories of the past, is not like solving an intellectual puzzle. It is a powerful, intensely personal healing moment. And it is no simple task. Particularly with childhood memories, the pain of them was overwhelming to the young child. As a matter of survival, intensely confusing and/or painful childhood experiences are often rapidly shunted off into unconsciousness; then a personality style develops in large part to keep it that way. Think of the common experience from childhood of the bully, the flincher, and the control freak. The humiliation and anxiety are the deepest and most inaccessible parts of their lives, kept unconscious because they were so intolerable and unwieldy at the young age at which they occurred.

These experiences are usually quite difficult for a person to remember; even once remembered they tend to slip repeatedly from awareness and have to be remembered all over again. That's one reason psychotherapy tends to take longer than a few sessions. Treatment requires making contact with exactly that which your defensive style, your personality – and later your symptoms – were developed to protect you from remembering. It requires facing your nightmares.

This phenomenon of avoiding awareness of painful experiences is called <u>resistance</u>. Like defenses, resistance is unconscious. It arises out of our defensive style and is no less central to our personalities. It is partly how we minimize distress and maximize mastery. The bully and the flincher have different defensive reactions to the same unpleasant childhood experience: The bully constantly does what was done to him, pushing at everyone and everything before they can hurt him; the flincher hides from the world in his fear of catastrophic humiliation from everyone around him. But these varied symptoms and defensive styles are serving the same goal – to avoid awareness of the experience, of the agony. These two reenact their original horror and their reaction to it (the flincher's avoidance or the bully's undoing/denial) in the safer context of current events; unconsciously, they lie – or shall we say, delude themselves – about what is happening to them.

If they entered psychotherapy, their styles of resisting the work would mirror the defensive styles of their personalities. The bully might shrug things off with casual bravado as we saw in "Bully"; or he might cover that defense with a façade of intellectual curiosity and great respect for psychotherapy – a façade he believes as he engages in it because again resistance is unconscious. The flincher might become apologetic and highly intellectualized, or may distract the sessions with irrelevant psychobabble which, superficially, seems to be a sincere effort to make good use of the session time. (Control freaks, I have found, use interesting combinations of all these approaches.)

Resistance is at the heart of psychotherapy. When we conquer it, the work is more than half over. In fact some schools of thought hold that "analysis of the resistance" is the therapy. This idea fits well with the point I made above that resistance is at the core of our personalities, that it is a product of the defensive style that is so basic to who we are. When we make contact with it, we have made contact with something at the heart of our true selves, and thus we will no longer be controlled by it.

As it is so central, we should not expect resistance to be limited to the realm of psychotherapy, any more than symptoms and defenses only appear in session. We do not resist painful material only in psychotherapy; we do it in all areas of our lives. Let's look at some examples of resistance, both in psychotherapy and in daily life.

My personal favorite came from a friend, Dave (not his real name), while we were seeing the movie "*Star Trek II*." Bear in mind that this is a man who can see a movie once and then quote extensive dialog, describe the sequence of shots that made up a scene, and hum the background music. In this movie, we find out early on that the hero, Captain Kirk, has an estranged adult son. During the scene in which this is discovered, I nudged Dave with my surprise about Kirk having a son. Oddly, Dave kept muttering "No, he doesn't." It was only at the end of the movie, after a scene in which father and son reconcile and hug, that Dave admitted Kirk had a son. He was understandably surprised by this blind spot. It's a startling error in someone as sharp and attentive as he is, especially while watching that movie. How could he sit in rapt attention and miss it?

In answering that question, remember again that it is logic and data that point the way, not preconceived notions about psychological issues. I suggest that Dave was in the throes of resistance not because I am the doctor but because all the data point straight to that conclusion. First, what about alternative explanations? Maybe he was distracted for a moment during the movie and simply missed it. Possible, but by his own admission, he wasn't missing a word; I saw him paying close attention; and even if both of us misread Dave and his attention did flag for a moment, isn't it odd that this happened at the exact moment when we discover Kirk has a son? Furthermore, and most glaringly, a momentary lapse in attention does not explain why he continued through several other scenes about this plot point to deny the existence of Kirk's son. To that you might say, "well he was annoyed with you, Doc, for interrupting the movie, so he just denied it to piss you off." Plausible from your point of view, but Dave is not someone who behaves in this way. If he were annoyed, he'd be more than comfortable saying, "Shut up, you're being a pest." (I know, because he's said it before.) Another alternative explanation is that maybe Kirk having a son was not made clear. If you saw the movie, you know that this development was very clear, repeated several different times by different characters. It was pretty hard to miss.

Having disposed of these more everyday explanations, we are left with three facts: 1) Dave never misses anything in the movies he sees; 2) he remained ignorant in the face of all the evidence that Kirk has a son; 3) there are no causes in present day reality for Dave's lapse. The only other place to look for answers is in the internal world, in Dave's psychology. The explanation that accounts for all of the data is that Dave resisted the idea of Kirk having a son. Unconsciously, he censored that information out of the movie. It was only in the final reconciliation scene when Kirk and his son hug that the real world evidence broke through his defenses and he had to acknowledge the truth.

This explanation is supported by some other facts. We know that as a child Dave wanted, like so many boys, to be Captain Kirk (he'd told me that); we also know that all boys at least at some point want to be like their fathers; and we know that all little boys crave a father figure, a perfect hero-parent.

Do you begin to detect an unconscious motivation? Dave didn't want Kirk to have a son because somewhere inside he fantasized that he was Kirk's son. Maybe this sounds odd and unnecessarily psychoanalytic but all the data point that way. This explanation also accounts for other things such as Dave's long standing obsession with *Star Trek* and especially with its hero over the years, and his forgiveness of William Shatner's more bizarre overacting when usually Dave is very impatient with such theatrical self-indulgences (he worked as a film critic for a while). These facts always suggested to me that *Star Trek* – and Captain Kirk in particular – meant something more to Dave than a diversion; they suggested that *Star Trek* was touching something much more central and powerful in his life, something that could overpower his intellectual, rational side. This is what happened so strikingly during the movie.

Most important as proof that resistance happened, was Dave's reaction; you may remember from the previous chapter that this is always the most important proof that we're on to something. The reaction was similar to that of a patient discovering something about himself during a psychotherapy session. The realization that he missed this central plot element and that he had a lot of powerful feelings about Kirk having a son brought out a plethora of associated thoughts and memories. He was surprised and quite emotional as he realized he'd always had a barely conscious fantasy of being the Captain's son, or perhaps protégé; in addition to his usual conscious fantasies from childhood of being the great Captain, he acknowledged more fleeting and disturbing ones of being the Captain's favorite. In a kind of flood of insight, he recalled moments of powerful disappointment with himself, his father, and their relationship, as well as a history of similarly troubled relationships with other male authorities and teachers over the years.

Notice, here, that Dave's insight was not intellectual. His first reaction was emotional, his feelings about Kirk having a son. Again, what counts is making contact with an experience, not with an intellectual concept. His subsequent thoughts about his own father were secondary to making contact with his powerful yearnings for a Kirk-father with whom he could have the ideal mentor-student, father-son relationship.

The fact that he has such a reaction is the proof that we have found something true about him. The entire topic resonated with Dave, it "clicked," and he described a sense of heightened awareness and wonder, as well as a rush of optimism. These reactions are a common occurrence in psychotherapy when the work is proceeding successfully. As with Dave, it is the product of insight, and it is one of the best signs that we are on the right track in our explorations.

Two important points about this example of resistance: First, like all defensive reactions it is an unconscious event. Had Dave been aware of his intense personal connection with Captain Kirk, he would have been surprised, disappointed, saddened by the news of Kirk's son – perhaps, being something of the bully, he would have reacted with derision – but he would not have missed it. Second, although unconscious and rather primitive and simple, his denial was quickly obvious to him and easily challenged. In someone with much more inner tension, greater anxiety, and a less solid sense of security, the resistance might have persisted longer or developed into something more complex and stubborn. We've already noted how easily children and even adults can start to believe the casual lies they tell themselves.

In psychotherapy, it can be very difficult to challenge even this simple and flimsy defense if only because of the subject matter. People are quite adamant about their denial, no matter how blatantly illogical. That applies not just to the little boy with crumbs on his face who claims he had no cookies but to also adults.

Greg told me in one of our early sessions about his 16 year old son's efforts to get a summer job. The boy had been unsuccessful in his search and Greg was getting worried. Greg worked in a school that had openings for summer assistants, no training or experience required. The family was living week to week, money was tight, and the son was talking about cars and college. Greg offered to help his son get a position at the school. According to Greg, his son's response was a rather disinterested "Nah," to which Greg then replied, "Well, then you aren't getting any spending money for next year." Combined with his tone of voice, it seemed obvious to me that Greg was, understandably, at least a little angry at his son, and probably hurt as well. He'd reached out to help, his son had responded negatively, and Greg had lashed out in return. But Greg insisted he had no such feelings. He maintained that his only motivation was "just to tell him the financial facts", and that his only feeling during and afterward was "some disappointment".

Just to be sure we're not engaging in groundless speculation, let's go over the logic: If all he wanted to do was inform his son of the financial realities, why did he say it with such a vengeful tone? He doesn't usually speak to his son or to anyone else with such rudeness. Nor is Greg a stupid man; he knows how to talk to people. He knows full well that such speech would only antagonize his son, decreasing the chance that he'd accept help with the job search and further poisoning their relationship. Finally, what else but resistance would blind this otherwise intelligent and reasonable man to what is so obvious to everyone else – his words and tone with his son are pretty indisputable evidence that he harbors more intense feelings than "some disappointment".

This kind of resistance is common in treatment, particularly at the beginning. It is partly why so many patients come for 3 visits or so and then quit. In psychotherapy, a person's awareness must be expanded to include thoughts, feelings, and behavior that were previously ignored, explained away, minimized in their import, or blocked out of awareness entirely; and many of these will be unsettling or unpleasant to discover.

Without this increasing awareness, there is no therapy. Consider how powerful Greg's resistance is. From the outside anyone can see this man is hurt and angry, or at least that he said something angry and cutting to his son. Yet Greg won't see it. Unless that changes, unless the therapist can get the patient to see aspects of his behavior and feelings that he is determined to avoid, there will be no progress. The patient will drop out of treatment, perhaps angered and insulted, perhaps simply bored that nothing seems to be happening in the sessions.

Now why specifically does Greg resist? At the simplest level it's unflattering to realize one harbors vengeful feelings towards one's son, and worse to see that these feelings are leaking out in conversation with him; how much more appealing and comfortable to interpret one's behavior as simple fatherly concern. (Remember, though, that this reinterpretation is an unconscious process.) Even more unsettling is the can of worms that is opened by awareness of even this simple incident. If Greg sees his true feelings and behavior in this exchange with his son, he becomes open to a host of similarly difficult and painful experiences. These include other moments of rage and hostility towards his son, other dissatisfactions with his life and his family, perhaps resentment of all the sacrifices he makes to support them, feelings of neglect and dismissal by them and by others in his life, consequent rage and hostility, earlier and more painful experiences of a similar nature; or maybe what's lurking is sorrow and emptiness that his son is growing up and will soon be gone; or maybe it's both. But to become aware of what happened inside him and between him and his son brings the risk of shaking up his whole experience of himself and his life, his whole "take" on everything. How much easier to just rewrite the scene so that he is simply a concerned father feeling "some disappointment".

And how powerful this resistance must be to protect him from so much. How dominant must it be in his personality, his daily functioning, for it to overwhelm awareness of even the simplest data – his words and tone towards his son, and the anger that he felt; similarly, how strong must resistance be to make my friend Dave miss so much in a movie he watched so intently. Resistance is this strong because it is a product of defense, and as we discussed in the last chapter defenses form the core of our personality. They develop early in life to protect us from being overwhelmed by our most painful and central experiences. They are long standing, deeply ingrained habits. Thus, Greg's resistance to awareness of what happened between him and his son was not new; as we subsequently found, it was the latest in a history of denying similarly painful and unsettling experiences.

Resistance is powerful and difficult to overcome because in confronting it we enter into the most protected, central areas of one's life. But it's here that we'll find the source of symptoms such as missing a movie happening in front of Dave's eyes, or Greg not noticing how nasty he was and how angry he felt. Now guess what Greg told me in our first session that he wanted from treatment: "Help getting along with my son". The area of is life he explicitly wants to explore and improve is that in which his resistance is strongest. He wants to learn about and improve his communication with his son, but it is as if every fiber of his being conspires to disrupt that learning. We resist most that which we want and need to see. This is exactly what makes psychotherapy such a difficult and quirky task for both patient and therapist.

Resistance works like friction, sending you in the exact opposite direction that you want to go. It's built into our defenses, our personality. So it will thwart not just psychotherapy but any effort to increase awareness. This is why efforts outside psychotherapy can be doomed to failure, and why new self-help books on age old subjects keep coming out. They books may not be bad – well, some are – but they cannot adapt and accommodate to your particular style of resistance, to your personality. There are times in our lives when we are open to new ideas that run counter to the demands of our resistance, as we saw with the woman I described at the end of chapter 1 who kept interrupting the bartender. But when we are not open – when resistance is high – the best self help book won't reach us. Our built in, unconscious resistance will be too strong. And again, as we saw with Greg and Dave, resistance is highest when the issue is most personal and central in our lives. Dave didn't miss anything in the movie except when his yearnings for a father were touched, something that is about as personal as things get. It's unfair, but the more we need to learn the material, the more powerful is our resistance to it and thus the less likely it is we will learn it.

Resistance is so intrusive because, like all defenses, it is unconscious. As such, it is out of our control. Greg and Dave could not by will power stop themselves from denying what is so plain to us. Indeed, from their point of view, they weren't denying anything in the first place. Greg's angry and hurt feelings were somehow deleted from memory, just as were his angry words and tone. Dave had no idea he had rewritten the *Star Trek* movie. From his point of view, I had misheard something; Captain Kirk didn't have a son and all references to that plot point were simply edited out of Dave's consciousness. We are usually this unaware of our resistance. As automatically as blood circulates, we rewrite history, our own lives, and the world around us to conform to the demands of resistance.

There has been some curious research findings along these lines over the years. It turns out that people in successful long term relationships are found to hold more illusory views of their partners than do other people. Also people who rate themselves happier are seen to maintain distorted views of themselves, others, and life. It seems, then, that resistance may have some survival value, that without at least a little denial we'd all sink into depression and get divorced.

Common Types of Resistance – I

When we first discussed his conversation with his son, Greg said to me, "I was just telling my son that I would not be able to help him next year." Even without thinking through the holes in this explanation, as described on pages 54 and 55, we know resistance is operating because Greg used one of my favorite give-away expressions. He said "I was just...." Often invariably when you hear someone start a sentence that way, you can be assured that they really mean quite the opposite. They weren't "just" anything; they were <u>very</u> something. Sometimes this is an unconscious undoing, as in Greg's case, other times not. We have all been subject to the indirect nastiness of someone who, when confronted, claims they were "just" something or other. Some people are consciously lying, some are honestly unaware of how hostile they are being, as Greg was. When unconscious, it is resistance.

When this arises in psychotherapy – denial of hostility – patient and therapist have some useful work to do. First the question must be resolved: Is the patient denying or minimizing something, i.e. resisting as Greg was, or is the therapist overreacting, being "too sensitive"? The answer, as always, is found in data. Just as we saw with Dave and Greg, there are usually ample facts and irresistible logic to point our way to the truth. To the extent that your therapist can help you see this road and you can travel it together instead of arguing back and forth, your treatment will be successful. As I said in chapter 1, you should be able to follow the process of a session into whatever strange territory it leads. On the other hand, even if your therapist is correct in his interpretations the therapy won't go anywhere unless he can show you in some palatable way. If I could not help Greg see that he was not "just telling" his son the facts but was venting some pretty strong feelings, the treatment would probably have stalled. More about this in the next chapter.

Resistance can take a form opposite to this kind of denial and minimizing, at least on the surface. Rather than minimize, some people will interpret, analyze, and expound upon all the hidden and varied significances and ramifications of something, but they do so in order to avoid something else, usually a more simple and painful truth. When you have that vague sense of insincerity as someone talks about himself, especially in the context of describing something unpleasant like a rejection or failure, look for this kind of resistance. In psychotherapy, if you find yourself expounding on theories of psychology and in particular on your own well-articulated inner conflicts, see if you're actually resisting something simple like "It hurts." This was the change we saw in Sandra and Bully (chapter 1).

A related form of resistance, one that is unfortunately common in daily life, is a retreat into an antagonistic and self-righteous stance (which the woman dealing with her boyfriend and the bartender in chapter 1 managed <u>not</u> to do). I used to see a patient at a nursing home who became greatly affronted when I asked her to repeat something she had mumbled. She would angrily insist that I was not listening, that I didn't care about her, that no-one did, and so on. When we could talk through these episodes, she would end up feeling much more relaxed. She would see that underneath these accusations lay the pain of loneliness in her old age, among other things. This in turn brought on reflection and regret about much of her past. When we talked about these issues her mood, her relationships with others including me, and her overall functioning would improve. When she suffered some assault to her physical condition and became more helpless, she would revert to this form of resistance again. It was shielding her from deeper, more confusing and disturbing pain. It was easier to be mad at me for being insensitive than to face the rest of her feelings about her aging, including the pain of family members not visiting her as often as she would have liked.

This kind of resistance occurs even in the most polite patients. Sara, age 38, saw me for about two years before she finally came out and acknowledged how accused she always felt when I said anything. She had made good progress for about a year and a half. She had become much less uptight and obsessive around men, she was able to walk away from casual encounters without the relentless replaying and re-analyzing that had plagued her at the beginning of treatment, she was less prickly and angry with her boss and colleagues, and she had broken some self-destructive habits in her relationships with her family and friends. But she could go no further with me. She had decided I was critical and rejecting, and I could find no way around this perception. Here is an excerpt from one of our last sessions. My attempts to let her vent her discomfort, to simply listen to her sympathetically, had gotten us nowhere, so I took a more active stance this time.

Sara: (politely, apologetic) Well, now I feel like I've wasted the session up to this point. I've been here all this time and still don't know how to get to the point.

Therapist: You get to the point often enough.

S: (pause) Well, now I know this is probably unfair, but it feels like you're patronizing me. You know I really did waste the time and can't get anywhere.

T: Yes, we've talked about that feeling you get that I'm patronizing you. But I promise I'm not. I tell you when I think you're stalling, don't I?

S: Yes, you do, actually. So you think I'm moving? (She said this with a sarcastic, tense smile.)

T: Yes.

S: (pause) So I'm wrong again?

T: Wrong? About what?

S: That I'm wasting session time, just stalling, getting nowhere.

T: Oh. No I don't think you're doing that.

S: Hmm. (Still with the tense, fixed smile.)

T: (lightly) What is this obsession with which of us is right? I mean, if I always agreed with you, there wouldn't be anything to learn here.

S: (pause) Well, then that's a bad thing you're saying I do.

T: Again, what's the obsession with whether you're being right, wrong, good, bad? How about the actual content of what we're talking about?

S: I can't remember now.

T: (For a moment, neither could I. This is a resistance we'll discuss in the next section of this chapter.) We were talking about whether you are opening up or still stalling.

S: O, yes.

T: Well, you've told me things lately you haven't been able to say before, and that's been happening with other people too, from what you say. (One of Sara's goals in therapy was to relax and communicate more openly with people so that she would not feel so chronically disconnected and lonely.)

S: (pause) Well, now it seems like it's me again.

T: What does?

S: Like it's always my fault I don't agree.

T: I'm sorry, I'm losing you; agree about what?

S: Whether I was wasting the session. It's my error to think that.

T: Yes, I suppose it is. But, Sara, I really <u>don't</u> feel like you wasted the first half of the session. I didn't think that conversation was useless or stalling. And as I say, it sounds like you've been talking more freely with other people, too.

S: See, it's like it's always my fault.

T: OK. So maybe you were "wrong" to think you'd been wasting the session. So what? Isn't it good news that you weren't?

S: (pause) See? It's me again. I'm always wrong.

T: Wait a second, here. Isn't that a relief, to know that you were not wasting session time, that you don't have to feel like you messed up?

S: But, see, I'm wrong, then, again. It's always me who did something or thought something that was wrong. See, I SHOULD be feeling relieved and I'm wrong to instead feel accused.

T: Again with the right/wrong. You look like you've been called to the principal's office.

S: It's very strong. It's always like you're telling me I'm wrong. Like I'm wrong to have that feeling, too. I can't do this anymore. I just know you think I'm wrong. And I'm not. (At this point I tried to remove myself from this debate and just listen, in the hope that she would vent her tension and remember again – as she really did know in her clearer moments – that I was not sitting in judgment of her. But she only continued in this vein.)

This almost reads like a comedy routine. I can't seem to say anything that comforts or calms Sara. I cannot find a way to usefully challenge, overcome, or dodge around the stance she has taken that "You're always accusing me, putting me down, and I can't do anything right in here!", although she was always very polite about it. Clearly it was time for Sara to stop treatment with me.

Notice that it does not matter in Sara's decision to stop treatment whether I was right in my interpretation of her behavior. It does not matter if she was, as I believe, enacting something from her past that had no justification in our actual relationship, something that was interfering with all her interpersonal relationships. Nor does it matter that I am sure she will need to become conscious of that reenactment, of the distortions she brings to her relationships – such as those she visited upon me – in order to move beyond her present state of anxiety, wariness, and isolation. These things don't matter to Sara, or to any patient in this situation, because I was unable to communicate them to her in a way that she would be able to hear and consider.

Not surprisingly, Sara left treatment soon after this session. She had cleaned up some of the more flagrant problems in her life, but she was unwilling – unconsciously – to explore any closer to the core of her difficulties. For some reason she had to avoid the meat of what in her feelings and her experiences led her to perceive accusation, to feel so self-conscious, and to behave the way she did; for although these symptoms had eased, they were still pronounced and caused her distress and interpersonal strife, as they did during our session. So she pulled away from me via this creation of an adversarial relationship. I could not find any way to break this cycle so quite rightly she left. If your therapist cannot help you to see what you're doing it makes little difference whether or not the therapist is the most acknowledged and revered expert in whatever ails you; the therapy still won't go anywhere.

Notice, by the way, that Sara's resistance was precisely the same as her defenses, as her symptoms. She struggled to overcome feelings of intense self-consciousness, to cease the relentless perception of accusation, to relax around people and have some trust in them and in herself. But she used this same <u>symptom</u> – perceived accusation and the constant belief that she is wrong – in service of <u>resistance</u>. This is a good example of how the path of psychotherapy can be so twisty and arduous. A symptom that Sara and I agree upon as something to conquer is also her mode of distancing herself and sabotaging the work.

II

In the middle of the Sara's session we both forgot what we were talking about. The confusion induced in both of us is another kind of resistance. The simplest example of this resistance is when you are confronted by someone and the only thought, feeling, or response you can find in yourself is "I'm confused". Upon later reflection, you might see no objective reason for the confusion, and you might realize you were immobilized by some mix of anger and fear. In any event, the confusion was a way of avoiding your own reactions. It is similar to the tactic of doubt and obsessing that we saw in Ron (see chapter 3).

Al told me of this symptom in himself when his wife was angry at him. It turned out that by becoming confused he was fleeing from some very dangerous feelings in himself – dangerous because taking note of them might lead to serious action, such as leaving or lashing out at her. Instead, the confusion kept him immobile. He did not argue back in any substantive way and he took no action that might change their relationship. He honestly felt unable to think clearly enough to do anything but acquiesce. The rage and disgust he felt towards her came out in our sessions. Those feelings were strong enough to scare him with the possibility that he might leave her, abandoning his daughter to whom he was very devoted, having to face all the unpleasantness and chaos of starting a new life. How much simpler it is to flee into confusion (unconsciously, of course).

In psychotherapy, confusion can be a powerful mode of resistance. It can be experienced by the patient or induced in the therapist, usually both, and it is always an unconscious tactic. You may recall that Ron exhibited this kind of resistance. Despite his high intelligence and considerable verbal facility – or more exactly, <u>because</u> of them – when we began to make some headway into his problems we would both become confused and distracted. (Of course the therapist has to be sure that his confusion is not the product of his own ignorance or lack of concentration. As always, data will point the way.)

Patients induce confusion or create it in themselves in many ways. Ron did it subtly and under the guise of providing additional and needed information. I had to catch him at this, then show him how irrelevant and distracting the information actually was. I had to get him to see that he was not helping us by offering additional information but was in fact actively trying to throw us off the topic. When I could do this, he would often at that point blurt out some painful experience or feeling that had been just at the edge of his consciousness, something he did not realize was eating at him until that moment. By the end of such a session, he always felt better.

This pattern of resistance and subsequent breakthrough of barely conscious material was always followed by improvement in his mood and functioning. This is what psychotherapy is all about. It is what you want from a session. Here is a more extended example of how it works.

Phil's style of resistance in psychotherapy was initially one of over intellectualizing everything. He would make lists of discoveries to talk over with me, most of which turned out to be red herrings. For example, he once came in and said he'd realized that his worries came down to 3 "key issues". One of them was that at the age of 38, he felt he'd not done enough with the past two decades. As soon as we pursued this line of thought, however, he admitted that he had done many things he'd wanted, accomplished a fair amount, and that "lots of people do less than I've done, and they feel OK about themselves." So his resume wasn't the issue after all.

Most important in this typical session with Phil was the confusion that ensued. He would come in with his lists and organized discoveries, but as soon as we began to follow any of them to some kind of conclusion, he would become lost and confused. Sometimes I did too.

At around session 15, he came in without such an agenda. He jumped from one worry to the next, such as "I've done nothing with my life," "I don't have a girlfriend to distract me from this pain," "I'm not doing enough with my career," "my mother's in debt," "maybe I should move out of her house, it's such a mess and much more work than I'd thought it would be," and more. (He'd moved into his mother's house to save money while he worked off some old debts.) During all this, I became as confused as he was, whereas in previous weeks I had felt a growing understanding of this man and his problems. I followed his meandering topics, trying to find one or more that seemed to have real impact on him, but in discussing them none held up as painful enough to cause his distress. His mother's debt was being taken care of, he had the money to hire people to help fix up the house or to move to an apartment of his own if he chose, his career was actually moving along quite well, and so on. Even his brother's possible relapse into drug abuse did not account for the tears that began to stream down his face as he talked.

Putting aside the anxiety this confusion was causing me – trying to have faith that it was a manifestation of Phil's resistance, not evidence that I should be selling storm windows for a living – I stopped Phil and asked him what moment, what thought, started the tears.

Phil: It's weird. It's so strong. I don't know.

Therapist: It looked like it started around the time you were talking about your mother's house.

P: (thinking) Yeah. The messy house.

T: The house.

P: I guess so.

T: Don't guess; remember.

P: I don't know.

T: You're the only one who does.

P: I guess I'm trying to give her the benefit of the doubt; I think a lot of this has been plateauing over the last few months and now she's like messed up... Well, the house was always like that. I mean, you can't blame your parents for everything. I don't know.

Notice how he suddenly scattered the focus off my question and into more chaotic generalizations. This was resistance – an attempt to confuse the issue, to flee the pain, anything but think and talk about himself. After a moment I asked him:

T: Where are you?

P: I'm in my head. I'm not in touch with anything. I'm confused.

T: Well, we know what confusion is.

P: (laughs) Yeah.

T: So back up. You were remembering where the tears started and talking about your mother and her house.

P: The fridge. (tears) Wow. It's the fridge. It's so fucked up. There's old food and mold and shit growing in there.

T: This feels like what hurts?

P: Yes.

T: Can you describe the hurt a bit? (Phil looks blank and shrugs.) Is it something you've felt before.

P: It's the same thing I felt when that woman I was running in the park with told me she was married.

T: Same as you felt when you thought your brother was relapsing?

P: Yes. No, that was more like anger. Also I was really tired. I don't really remember that moment.

T: [It seems we've broken through the confusion on both sides of the room. He's clearer about what hurts and I hear a familiar theme – tears triggered when he feels left behind to his dreary "fucked up" home/life. Let's see if it flies.] When else have you had that feeling?

P: O, man, all the time. Every time a woman breaks up with me. No, actually it's any time I see a woman, or anyone, who I think has their life together.

From here, Phil went on to relate more memories of feeling left behind, left out. At the end of the session he was talking about the refrigerator of his childhood, how it and the whole house were such a mess, how he could never find anything to eat, his embarrassment bringing friends over, how he felt his brother was much favored over him. The flood of memories and insight coupled with a surge of energy tells us we are on the path to the real issues.

Phil recalled during this session that earlier in the week he'd felt brushed aside by a colleague at work, and that this was where his bad mood started. This triggering incident was forgotten and, sure enough, he began the session grasping at any fact as proof of his hopeless inadequacy. This is what we saw in Fred and Carl in chapter 1. Phil was enacting the role that this event reinforced: The loser from the pathetic home. All the stories in the early part of the session, all the confusion, were in service of that role. The confusion was resistance to remembering the pain of that role – first at home with the refrigerator and all the memories attached to it, then in the present (triggered by his mother's still chaotic and depressing refrigerator), and most recently with his colleague at work.

Now surely that event of his being brushed off at work didn't cause all the tears. It was closer to the mark than the earlier material he brought in, but it couldn't cause such pain by itself. No, that triggering event was itself a product of resistance. It was used unconsciously as a less painful version of a more agonizing memory – the memory of childhood abandonments, of being brushed off as a child by his family, and of the general sense of chaos and despair that was associated with the memory of the refrigerator. How do we know this? Again, data. First, the events that Phil described do not cause the degree and depth of pain he showed in my office. Second, Phil himself could sense that this triggering event (at his job) was not at the heart of the matter.

Third, when Phil told me of the event in detail it turned out that the colleague had not brushed him off at all! What happened, then? Like Dave rewriting the *Star Trek* movie, Phil rewrote the interaction at work in accordance with his long-standing pattern of expecting and deserving rejection. He not only fixated on a rather trivial rejection in the present, but in fact invented that event to distract himself from deeper pain. This is what we saw above with Sara and the nursing home resident inventing and then fixating on something I supposedly did to make them feel so bad.

What we don't remember, we are doomed to act out, said Freud. Or, as they say in another arena, those who remain ignorant of history are destined to repeat it.

Phil's is a good illustration of the complexity of resistance. All the myriad ways he denigrated himself and his life at the beginning of the session were resistance – they were an enactment of a forgotten incident from only a few days back. But that incident was itself used as resistance to even more painful experiences. Defenses, resistance, symptoms build on each other in this way, layering over and over. Phil was of course unaware of all this – the rewriting of the encounter at work, the enacting of an old childhood script in the process, the layering over with yet another level of resistance by enacting that encounter via his demeanor in my office, his forgetting the incident at work. Like all resistance, these are unconscious events so the illogic of it all escaped him.

Phil would remain locked in these reenactments, honestly feeling worthless and seeing proof of it everywhere he turned, until we were able to break through his resistances. At that point he could remember both the secondary source of the pain – the imagined brush off at work – and the more distant and primary experiences which originally gave him this script, the ones that really caused him to go through his life expecting and perceiving desolation. By the end of the session, he felt much clearer and saner, although he was understandably quite sad. Still, as one patient once put it, "better sad than crazy".

Breaking through resistance led to a great deal of buried material resurfacing and Phil could then stop enacting the role he was brought up with, a role that left him miserable and confused. Unfortunately, one breakthrough does not a treatment make. It must happen repeatedly because resistance is like habitual bad posture – as soon as you relax, it tends to creeps back in without your noticing.

Resistance, like symptoms, can be a compromise between conflicting needs at the core of our personalities; it serves both masters. Phil's over-intellectualizing was his best compromise between maximizing mastery and minimizing pain. Think about this. While he rallies his intellect at the conscious level in service of the first agenda, trying to understand and conquer his despair by figuring out the best course of action for his life, he unconsciously uses that same intellectual prowess in the service of the second – he flees the pain by confusing the very issues he wants and needs to understand. Here, then, is "why psychotherapy". Here is why self analysis, even with the help of books, workshops, friends, etc., is so tricky: Your resistance will conspire to blind you to exactly that which you are trying to see.

III

Look back for a moment at the ninth line of the excerpt from Phil's session. I asked him what thought started the tears as he talked; he equivocated and then answered, "I'm trying to give her (his mother) the benefit of the doubt...." This is an example of another defense common in psychotherapy and in life. If you can learn to catch it in yourself you will save a lot of time in treatment. If you can catch others doing it, you'll know when you're being led off the track into confusion or into some agenda other than your own. It is the defense of, quite simply, not answering what was asked. In psychotherapy it takes a few very specific forms. Most commonly it consists of answering the question "what do you feel?" with something that begins "I think" or "He/she/it/they..."

I asked Jill what she felt about her boyfriend during their current difficulties. She answered "he's having a hard time." That is not what I asked. I repeated, "No, what do you feel about him, not what do you judge his current life situation to be." After some hemming and hawing she answered, "Angry! Deprived. I wish he didn't have his damn problems." At this point Jill's bitchy behavior towards her boyfriend – which she had been reluctant to acknowledge – made sense: She was whiny and bitchy towards him because she had those feelings about him.

Right about now you might be saying the same thing that Jill did: "But that's so unfair. I've no right to feel that way. His job woes are a real problem for him; I should be understanding." This is another form of resistance. It is similar to what I warned against in chapter 1 where you might find yourself saying "that's ridiculous, why would I do/feel/think/ say that?" Jill herself christened it "Retreat into the Concrete".

She was quite right that her bitchy behavior was unreasonable. But however unreasonable and unjustified her behavior was, however unfair or selfish her feelings were, the fact remains she did have those feelings. Telling me, and herself, that the poor man is having a "hard time" only serves to avoid this fact. It is, therefore, resistance. It is very much like the resistance of overanalyzing I mentioned a few pages back. I said that if you catch yourself expounding at great length, it might be that you are avoiding simpler and more painful facts about your experience. In Jill's case, she resisted the facts that 1) she resented her boyfriend, and 2) she showed it.

These truths hurt; it is much easier for Jill to dwell on "I shouldn't be bitchy towards him" than to acknowledge just how bitchy she did feel, especially since she did not believe her boyfriend deserved such treatment. This awareness requires further that she examine why and whence cometh such selfish feelings and behavior, it requires opening those worm cans. Does Jill feel and act that way in other relationships? on the job? If she is not usually this unreasonable a person, what is fueling such selfish feelings and behavior with her boyfriend? Better to avoid the whole topic; just admit to the doctor that she's behaving selfishly, apologize to her boyfriend, and especially never face the question "how do you feel about him?" This is what she tried to do.

The trouble is that it doesn't work to pretend a feeling isn't there. It will surface again, if not in bitchiness, then in some other symptom. Maybe Jill will start hating her boyfriend's apartment or his voice, maybe she will start hating herself, maybe she will develop an obsession with searching out and destroying "selfishness" in herself or others. Almost anything is possible in the realm of defenses and symptoms, but rest assured the feeling will out.

(Of course, before any of the above work with Jill, we would have to consider the possibility that she was <u>not</u> being bitchy to Frank. We would have to discuss exactly what was said between them and evaluate whether her feelings and behavior really do qualify as "bitchy." But since she and I had worked together for 2 years, I could skip that step; I already knew that Jill's style was hardly one of assuming the worst in her own behavior. On the contrary, she tended to soft-pedal her contribution to the strife in her relationships. So if she says she's been bitchy, we can believe it.)

This "retreat into the concrete" is most apparent when patients insist, "That's stupid. It doesn't make sense. Why would I feel that way." Greg, who barked with vengeance at his son, was doing this. He said, "I was just (!) telling him the financial facts. Why would I be mad at him? He's just (!) shy. No 17 year old wants to take a job from his old man...." This is very reasonable, admirable, and understanding on Greg's part but it is also completely false, a retreat to the concrete. He <u>was</u> mad at son, and he showed it. And of course there is that second "just". You can bet that shyness is the last thing he believed to be motivating his son's words. On the contrary, he felt rejection and dismissal from his son; and his son may indeed have had this in his voice. As soon as you hear yourself saying "Why would I do/feel/think that? That's silly," back up and re-ask the question "What <u>did</u> I actually do/feel/think?"

This resistance can rise to quite an absurd level. Susan was a 16 year old girl who showed all the symptoms of a lifelong attention problem. Her mind raced constantly, she obsessed, and despite her high intelligence was often behind in school. She wanted very much to work with me and was fascinated by the process, yet her mind kept jumping to every distraction, whether something in the office or in her own thoughts. It is a well documented fact that several medications work wonders with this kind of problem. They enable the person to experience a clarity and focus of concentration and attention that they had previously thought unattainable. Yet, when I suggested this to Susan she could not get past the notion that "I just don't see how a pill can change how you think." This was not the adolescent bravado that one often sees; Susan was beyond such posturing during our sessions. She honestly could not fathom the possibility. It was as if she was told that gravity exists, shown how a ball rolls down a hill, yet maintained, "How can something be invisible and pull the ball down the hill; that's preposterous." The superficial logic this position serves to avoid awareness of very obvious facts.

A related form of resistance was given a wonderful name by another adolescent patient I saw. She called it "Hairsplitting the Irrelevant." You can probably guess how this one works. It's just like a retreat into the concrete except that it goes farther. In this resistance, the patient elaborates on minute and trivial specifics. If Jill were to insist on explaining that her boyfriend was having a hard time not because it was so hard to find a job in the current market but because he's got very specific skills and is in fact overqualified blah blah blah, she would be "Hairsplitting the Irrelevant." These statements not only don't change the fact that she resents him, but in words like that you can hear her trying to talk herself out of what she feels. As Shakespeare put it, "the lady doth protest too much".

IV

Something else one often hears in psychotherapy is "I already know about my life, my childhood. I remember what happened and I know how it affected me. Why dredge it all up?" We heard that from "Bully" and Sandra in chapter 1. Such resistance is the result of a defense called "isolation". This important defense turns up in many forms of minor and severe psychological difficulty. Freud was the first to describe it.

Let's back up first and discuss in what context this statement would be resistance and not the simple truth about the person. Remember, now, we are not talking about someone who's doing just fine – such people do exist and do remember their (usually benign) childhoods; no, we're talking about a person who has symptoms. First, as all the examples in this chapter have shown, people do not know when they are resisting. The very nature of resistance is that it keeps you unaware that there is a problem. Second, I often hear it long before I've even begun to think about someone's childhood; as I mentioned at the beginning of this chapter and will discuss in more detail in the next chapter, psychotherapy does not always require exploration into the past. Why the defensiveness that you will be asked about it? Third, and I must ask you to take this somewhat on faith if it is not clear by now, virtually none of us can know our childhoods. The simple fact that we have a personality is a testament to the existence of defenses; defenses exist because at least some of our childhood experiences had to be defended against, avoided, forgotten. One of the most important and popular books in the world of clinical psychology is Alice Miller's *Prisoners of Childhood*. In it she quotes the "first commandment of childhood: Thou shalt not be aware." I refer you to this excellent book for further discussion of this fact that very few of us can really remember our childhoods. Finally, and here's the kicker, if a person truly remembered their childhood, and all its pains and pleasures, then why do they have symptoms? Symptoms come out of the defenses that make up our personalities, defenses which develop to protect us from painful experiences. When those defenses grow rigid, exaggerated, or otherwise out of our control, it can only be because something unconscious is irking us. In other words, there is something we don't remember.

How do we account for the fact that some people do seem to remember childhood. How can someone who remembers important childhood scenes still be resisting, still have symptoms? For indeed many people do fit into this category. The answer is <u>isolation</u>. The person has isolated out the affect (the emotion) from those memories. He may remember the scene, but he has forgotten the experience, the feel of it. "Bully" in chapter 1 is an excellent example of this phenomenon. It is quite common actually that we can recall a scene, an event, even quite vividly, but the impact of that scene and the specific pain or pleasure it caused are largely forgotten. This is a necessary defense in early childhood, common to all children. Remember I pointed out in chapter 1 that something which is a mild irritant to an adult may be intense and overwhelming to a small child. Well, no one can survive being overwhelmed all the time. The defense of isolation protects a child from the intensity of experience while preserving "just the facts" of that experience. This is why I said at the beginning of this chapter that there was a crucial difference between my thesis here and what I heard from the radio psychologist. That psychologist seemed to focus more on those facts, on the details of the patterns of reenacting old family scenarios. But because of isolation, one can indeed see those patterns and yet continue in painful and self-defeating behavior and feelings. Without contacting the <u>experience</u> of a memory, that memory is not going to be of much use. That is why the people who say "I already remember it all" are usually not feeling any improvement from the work.

You can see the resistance of isolation most easily in yourself. Think of those odd distant memories that we find are for some reason as vivid as whatever is right in front of our eyes at this moment. We often don't see why these have remained so clear and alive, they may seem quite unimportant, yet there they are. What is happening is that the affect associated with the memory – the experience – has at least in part been isolated, shunted out of awareness, forgotten.

Unconsciously, however, those feelings are still alive. That is what is fueling the memory. Unconscious feelings are, like all feelings, energetic, part of our personal life force if you will. That energy keeps the memory alive where other, less emotionally loaded memories, fade deeper into the unconscious or are forgotten altogether (no one really knows what happens to them).

How do we know this is so, that the memories are laced with unconscious feeling? By now you should be saying it out loud with me: Data. First, something has to be keeping those memories alive; otherwise they would fade like all the others. Second, when in psychotherapy those memories come up and can be explored fruitfully, lo and behold the forgotten – isolated out – affect returns to them. The patient usually has a strong feeling, deep in the gut, that we have hit a truth about himself, that we have found a buried treasure. He can remember why the memory was important in the first place. Most important, that memory with all its restored emotion often logically accounts for or at least plays a major part in the present day behaviors and feelings which brought him into treatment. We saw that Bully's forgotten experience in the office with his father was a model for how he moved through his whole life. Finally, when this material surfaces, the patient experiences a release of tension, a surge of energy, and often a flood of related memories and insights, and he feels saner and clearer. In short, the positive effects we want out of a psychotherapy session are accomplished in the process of exploring this seemingly unimportant story that for some hitherto unknown reason stuck in the memory. (Sometimes, these memories even become a cornerstone of the entire course of treatment. I will explain this further in the next chapter, in the section on screen memories.)

When isolation turns up in psychotherapy, it often occurs in the following way. You, a relatively new patient in your first 10 or 20 sessions, will tell a story. That story will be told as perhaps a mildly upsetting event, if told with any emotion at all. But the story may have a remarkable impact on the therapist. He experiences all the impact that you have isolated out of awareness. You talk about an encounter with someone, and the therapist finds himself unaccountably enraged, claustrophobic, or depressed. This is a powerful experience in a psychotherapy session. If the therapist can show you the missing emotion, if he can give it back to you to experience and process for yourself, great progress can be made.

Isolation is strongest in the context of our childhoods. This should not come as a surprise. Remember that resistance is strongest to issues that are most central and emotionally loaded for us. Surely little is more central in carries more emotional weight than experiences from our childhoods, when we were most dependent on others, most defenseless, most needy. Surely that is when things hurt, and please, most acutely.

And isn't it more than coincidental that this aspect of psychotherapy — tracing things back to one's childhood — is often the most lampooned in the media, as well as the most dreaded and rejected by new patients? You have probably heard people tease about psychotherapists teaching you to "blame it all on your parents"; you may have resisted discussion of your past in your own treatment on these grounds.

By the way, psychotherapy is not about blaming your parents or anyone else. When we discuss the past, the point is to increase awareness of what happened and what effect it had on you so that you can be free from those experiences and live more of the life you want. At least at the beginning, it doesn't particularly matter whether you were an insatiable brat or your parents were cold, withholding people; what matters is what you experienced, how you interpreted and adapted to it, and how it continues to interfere with your current life. Think about the chronically deprived and depressed complainer who cries in agony that his friends are not supportive enough. It may be that he has picked very selfish friends. It may be he asks the impossible. In either case, why can't he see the self-destructiveness of choosing such friends or expecting too much? Because he is enacting some agenda, some scenario, from the past. He needs to remember that original experience. Then he'll be able to see what he is doing. Then he'll know, probably without much input from me, if his is — and was — hopelessly demanding of life or a doormat who chases the wrong people. (Some writers take this point even a step farther and point out that the issue of who is to blame is rarely resolved anyway — who is to say what constitutes "insufficient nurturing", "too demanding", "too sensitive", and so on?)

Isolation turns up in all of us, but is most pronounced in several severe conditions. People with obsessive disorders rely heavily on this defense. It is also central in many of the more severe dissociative disorders, in which people experience altered states of consciousness, such as multiple personality disorder (now called Dissociative Identity Disorder), paranoia, and schizophrenia. But it is quite ubiquitous in less troubled people; keep your eyes open and you'll see it frequently.

V

Finally, here's one of my pet examples of resistance. Isn't it amazing how the same people who know the contents of every last diploma and certificate on their podiatrist's wall (and I've seen offices with 15 such documents) cannot tell you anything about their therapist beyond a name? They know all about the expert who treats their feet, but nothing about the person who deals with their heads and hearts. You ask if this person in whom they are entrusting their most private and profound thoughts and feelings is a psychiatrist, psychologist, social worker, or what, and they don't know. You ask if the therapist is licensed, and if so as what; again they don't know. You ask if the therapist has had special certification or training in particular areas, and they can't tell you. In fact at this point they probably tell you to lighten up. Clearly there is some kind of resistance going on because the data do not point to any other conclusion. These are not patients who normally remain blissfully ignorant of such matters; quite the contrary.

Of course, resistance is never simple: The opposite behavior can be a product of resistance as well. Sometimes patients insist on all the "right" credentials before daring to talk to a therapist. They must have a male, or a cognitive therapist, or an eating disorder specialist, or someone who is himself recovering from drug or alcohol abuse, or an expert who has done research into compulsive hand washing, or whatever. I will explain in the next chapter why these concerns are usually irrelevant (see "Choosing a Therapist"). For the moment here is an example of how they are used in service of resistance. The respected psychoanalyst James Masterson wrote a book on the treatment of borderline personality disorder. The book was very well received, not only by the academic and clinical community but by the public. He was suddenly besieged by far more patients than he had time to see, all requesting psychoanalysis with this expert. He referred them to colleagues. He later found out that very few of them ever contacted those colleagues for treatment. I'd bet my right arm that Masterson would agree that his colleagues were competent to treat those patients. But the patients used the need to see the absolute expert in service of resisting the treatment. One moment these people are reaching out for help, the next they have found a reason to retreat again. (Because someone once asked me, I feel compelled to point out that this story is not told in the spirit of sour grapes; I am not one of the colleagues to whom Masterson referred his patients.)

Conclusion

I had a difficult time writing this chapter. In reading the final version, I was still unsatisfied: I simply could not get the text as clear and yet comprehensive as I wanted it to be. I finally stopped rewriting when I accepted that the problem is the subject matter. Resistance is a very thorny, complicated, and persistent phenomenon in psychotherapy and in life. It creeps into our lives in many forms, often quite subtly, and it happens outside of our awareness. I am left describing something, therefore, that is often invisible, sometimes destructive, usually counterintuitive, and as far reaching in its effects as an unchecked computer virus.

It is resistance that blocks us from simply learning what we need to learn and then putting it to use, as we can do with a math lesson. Resistance in fact prevents our seeing not only what we need to learn, but also that we need to learn; it blocks our seeing that there is anything wrong. Recall that Greg (page 55) maintained that his outburst of resentment towards his son never happened, that he was just telling his son the facts and that he had no hostile feelings towards the boy. Were it not for resistance, which is a bit like saying "Were it not for our personalities", Greg would not deny what he did and felt. If not for defenses and resistance, we would not be subject to irrational and destructive moods and behavior, we would not hurt the ones we love nor be drawn to those that hurt us; and there would be a very small and highly regarded group of self-help books that we would all use to solve life's difficulties.

But our struggle for inner peace and for sanity in our lives is fraught with resistance. It sometimes seems that all the books in the world, all the support groups, and all the love of our friends and family cannot help. When we most need them we are most resistant to their help, and at such times usually most blind to the issues that cause us the greatest problems.

At these times when resistance is strongest, we are most lost, most stuck, and most lying to ourselves. That is when we can least comprehend and control our behavior, our feelings, our relationships, even our thoughts. We say we want to change, but things keep happening the same way, or the changes seem to backfire or take us in even more uncomfortable directions. We repeat and reinforce to ourselves that there is nothing rational to our fears, yet we remain afraid. We swear to listen to and absorb what a therapist or spouse or best friend is trying to tell us, then find ourselves berating those people with the greatest contempt and superiority for their moronic notions. Or, as Carl (chapter 1) so often did, we simply "forget" everything that was discovered and <u>experienced</u> last session and start the next one as if a beginner. We swear never to let another person control us, then turn around and get into another masochistic relationship. We face the fear, we believe, then panic at the next elevator, rush to the stove to check it yet again, or become tongue tied at the next mild confrontation. At these times resistance – unconscious motivations, feelings, and agendas – is interfering with our conscious desires; and we can't even see how it happened. That is "why psychotherapy".

CHAPTER 6

TREATMENT

By now three things should be clear if I've done my job. 1) Resistance won't go away by will power. Something else is required. 2) Feelings and behavior are changed in psychotherapy by expanding one's awareness (which is why the term "shrink" is so silly). 3) In exploring what is wrong in our lives the key is not remembering who did what to whom but remembering emotional experience; we may trace symptoms and resistance back to their roots in childhood because that is where they came from, but that is secondary to connecting with experiences, past or present.

What is Psychotherapy?

We stop being lost, we become unstuck, by increasing our awareness at a level beyond the intellectual, by exposing the lies. Psychotherapy is the process that accomplishes this. It enables us to change undesirable feelings, thoughts, and actions by increasing our awareness of our thoughts, feelings, actions, perceptions, and, if necessary, our pasts. It is only via such awareness that we can see what is troubling us and begin to behave, think, and feel differently. With very few exceptions, all psychotherapies work in this way. The exceptions are discussed later on in this chapter.

Symptoms begin with defenses which are established at an unconscious, emotional level; therefore so, too, must the treatment reach into this level. Intellectual learning is rarely enough and can even be a distraction. The deeper learning is often referred to as <u>insight</u>, a word that has, unfortunately, fallen out of vogue. The difference between insight and other kinds of learning are at the heart of psychotherapy.

Evan was struggling with the idea of breaking up with his wife. He could not make the decision because of an immobilizing fear that he would lose contact with his 5 year old son, even if the couple had joint custody. His wife was not likely to contest custody or visitation, both parents were settled in their community and planned to live close by so the child could easily stay at either one's home. She was not pressuring their son for his loyalty and to reject Evan (parental alienation). Evan had been attending some support groups and had discussed such concerns, the fear of losing the family, of being alone, of missing the spouse regardless of how horrible the relationship had become, and of losing one's children in a battle for their affections. A friend of his pointed out that the quality of his time with his son, even if it declined by a few days each week, would probably improve because his wife would not be there. She was a tense, at times rather frantic woman and had some trouble being calm around the family because she knew her husband no longer loved her. Of all this counsel, however, Evan said "I don't know, it just don't cut it. I don't feel any better. I still get really shaken by the idea of leaving and I can't see how it would work. I'm sure I'd lose my son. But that's preposterous," Evan would then say; "I know that; he knows his mother is a sweet but silly woman and he's never taken anything she says in her crazy moods to heart." He'd go back and forth like this each session, then he'd sit rather sheepishly, apologetic for repeating himself so much, and often make some little, self-effacing joke about it. Bear in mind Evan was not typically indecisive. He worked in law enforcement, was a firearms instructor, a biker, a mountain climber, and he led wilderness trips for kids and adults; it was not his style to be a worrier.

I met his son and the boy was just as Evan described. He was relaxed and thoughtful with a wisdom and gravitas beyond his years. He told me that he loved his mother and knew that she was not to be taken seriously when she got excited or when she talked about Evan. Grinning affectionately he continued that "She's really fun but she gets like that: I don't listen to her when she starts up complaining about Dad, or anything else."

Evan was lying to himself when he kept insisting that he knew his son would not drift away from or turn against him if the parents separated. There was a deeper lie as well having to do with his own profound self-doubt, despite all of his self-assurance in other areas. He began to see that in fact he believed his son would quickly and effortlessly forget him because he was profoundly forgettable. I'll discuss in more detail how we exposed those lies below, see "Types of Psychotherapy". For now let me just describe the result of catching them.

Once he became aware of what was really going on inside him, the change was striking. Previously hesitant, apologetic, and vague, he now spoke with strength and in clear and complete sentences. Rather than sitting huddled in a corner of the couch, he sat up and took command. Most important, these gains sustained outside my office. He began to think rationally about his family situation and soon made a decision; he was no longer stuck in anxiety and confusion.

The realization that gave Evan such liberation and clarity was personal, emotional, and felt like the lifting of a great weight. "I feel it in my bowels" was his colorful description. This is what I mean by insight. To the extent that his friend's counsel and the support groups were calming, comforting, and accurate, they were therapeutic. But these did not reach beyond the intellectual level. The kind of intensely personal and energizing insight that Evan experienced in session is what should be happening in psychotherapy.

The road to greater awareness is different for every course of psychotherapy. Patients take different roads into and out of the lies, and they do not respond to the same techniques. We want both the bully and the flincher to become more aware of their motives and underlying feelings of humiliation and impotence so that they need not use such disruptive behavior to defend against those feelings in daily life. But these two may require very different styles, as we saw in the last chapter (as we also saw in chapter 1 where we contrasted the different roads taken by the patients in *Good Will Hunting* and *Ordinary People*.) Treatment will progress for each according to his own comfort level, depending on a lot of environmental and personal factors that may be pressuring them to change, and only in so far as a therapist can help them make contact with unconscious and highly uncomfortable material.

And because this process and the content of the discussions are so personal, the success of the treatment is highly dependent on the relationship between a particular patient and his particular therapist. The therapist must of course be someone who's expertise is valued and trusted, but that trust must extend far beyond these dry areas; the therapist must be someone with whom the patient can examine the most private and uncomfortable aspects of himself, from whom he can hear input about these difficult areas. This is unlikely to happen unless the patient can experience the therapist as emotionally connected to him, as having his own personality. We may crave an emotionally reserved expert for troubles with our bones, intestines, or taxes, but few of us can drop resistance and attain insight in such impersonal relationships; we need the ideal friendship that psychotherapy provides. Otherwise it's too easy for what the therapist says to be dismissed, too easy to fall back into old habits of resistance.

In my first year of graduate training, I was seeing a 36 year old inpatient at a state psychiatric hospital. This man was taking a daily dose of antipsychotic medication 10 times larger than the dose that would put you or me into a sound sleep for 24 hours, yet he still walked around with tight muscles, various nervous tics, and his face in a tense squint. His habitual resistance in sessions was confusion and a retreat into the concrete. To the simplest of statements he would say something like "I don't know what that means. Does that mean... or is it ...?" and so on. One day, this man admitted in passing that he felt "like a criminal." "Like a criminal?" I asked. He immediately began his litany of "Well, I don't know what a criminal is. Is a criminal someone who... or is it ...." This time I impulsively interrupted with, "Oh, come on, John, you just used the word; you know what it is." I expected violence or a psychotic breakdown, but John just looked at me for a moment (he often stared at the floor while we talked) and then said, "Yes, I do."

I was worried by my impulsive and almost irritated statement, especially since I'd not yet read or heard of any therapist behaving that way. I was in my first year of training, just barely understanding how to listen and keep my mouth shut during a session. In those days, I went over every moment of every session with supervisors and I reviewed this one as well. To my surprise, my supervisor didn't disapprove of what I'd done. Instead he told me, "When the relationship is there, you can say almost anything."

John responded quite well to this relationship, proving what my supervisor had said. Early in our work he told me that he was so physically tense because were he to relax "buildings would come crashing in, bridges would fall, fires would burn." We never discussed this point further, but towards the end of treatment (about 6 months later), the same question arose of why such tension in his body. This time John's answer was "I might get crazy, break things, smash windows." These answers show a progression from a psychotic perception of the world, in which his feelings can cause distant buildings to fall, to the more commonplace fear of losing control of himself.

Actually, it should be no surprise that the relationship is so crucial to psychotherapy, and that one patient's relationship with his therapist might be vastly different from another patient's relationship with the same therapist. In the last chapter we saw how resistance can be so powerful, pervasive, and stubborn. We saw how it is rooted in the basic defenses which form our personality, and upon which we rely to get through life. A person would need a rather special circumstance in order to become aware of that resistance. He would need a unique, safe, and special environment in which he can dare to drop the defenses and realize what he truly feels, thinks, and does, and what truly goes on – and went on – in his life. Few of us get to do this even with our closest friends. Psychotherapy has always been burdened with practitioners who try to take the relationship out of it, starting with the early followers of Freud and continuing today with the talk of "scientific" or "evidence based" treatments (don't hold me to the lingo; it changes yearly). But it has never really worked. Although perhaps not fashionable, sexy, "scientific", or otherwise impressive as a concept, the relationship counts.

Compare the treatment of 2 adolescent boys, both about 14 at the start of treatment, both with similar behavior problems – cutting school, failure to comply with rules at home and in school (when they went), heavy marijuana smoking. They were both sullen, unresponsive, with few interests and a limited social life, and both were of similar intelligence levels and came from single parent families with emotionally distant fathers. Yet in treatment they developed quite different relationships with me, and went through very different paths to change.

Patrick was unresponsive to adults except when he exploded in violence at which times he would commit minor acts of vandalism. Those acts damaged his own property as often as it did others'. In the past he had exhibited behaviors that marked him as a very poor prospect for any kind of successful adjustment. He had been cruel towards animals and he used to bang his head on the lockers at school to get attention. He had been hospitalized twice for such disturbing behavior. Statistics show that children with histories like this often do not respond to psychotherapy and end up in jail or worse.

Patrick's behavior was irrational; he damaged his prize drums as readily as he stole his mother's five-dollar bills. He admitted enjoying the latter behavior, and the marijuana, but acknowledged his confusion over why he would wreck his own property. In one of his few utterances during first months of treatment he was painfully articulate about being lost. Of his outbursts, he said, "I can't stop it. It just happens. I don't know why". Patrick's mother was very confused as to where to draw the line with her son's behavior, and how to enforce her wishes once she decided on that line.

Patrick's father was an alcoholic who had moved out of the house just before I met Patrick. Apparently, at a family meeting at the hospital, father was pressured by therapists and his wife to stop drinking; Patrick spoke up about resenting it as well. Father said he wasn't about to give up drinking, and he left.

Patrick was blank, listless, almost zombie-like during our early sessions. If a patient doesn't relate to you in some way, even if non-verbally, you can't have a relationship. No relationship, no psychotherapy. So I brought his mother in and the three of us talked about what was needed for the household to be sane, functional, and under appropriate adult control rather than her son's. Patrick didn't contribute but at least he heard the process. Mother was very unsure of herself, and I ended up being a kind of surrogate authority figure in the house for a while. She called me frequently to ask if she was handling things well.

During that year, Patrick was sent to the hospital, to court, and eventually to long term placement because he was so out of control at home. He called me several times from placement, and finally change began to happen. When he returned home, he slowly became a real psychotherapy case. We began to talk about things; we uncovered feelings, thoughts, and especially behaviors of which he was previously unaware; we saw together how his father's attitude and behavior over the years had so perplexed and hurt him; we discovered all the myriad feelings and attitudes that were causing his various behaviors. By the end of treatment, he had developed a life full of diverse activity, none of which was destructive, a girlfriend he stayed with for over two years, and a new circle of friends; he was energetic and engaged, and he was rapidly turning into a responsible adult.

Over the years, Patrick's sessions were full of resistance. At the beginning of treatment he flat out refused to deal with me. Later his resistance took on more subtle forms. Even years into our relationship, he had a habit of treating me and our conversations as if he were being interrogated by a hostile school principal. (This is the resistance of assuming an antagonistic stance that was discussed in the previous chapter.) Sometimes, we could both see this resistance as a reaction to quite agonizing self-consciousness and feelings of inadequacy – it was easier to make an enemy of me than to experience those horrible feelings. Other times, we couldn't get anywhere. Meanwhile, I had to strike a balance between being the stern authority he and his family needed, and providing the understanding, support, and guidance that would allow him to get beyond his pose of disinterested hostility. I had to confront harshly yet remain accepting and sympathetic, helping Patrick and his mother articulate the many confusing feelings, thoughts, opinions, and frustrations that were entangling their lives. I think I talked more in my sessions with Patrick than I did with any other patient. Contrast that with Mike's course of treatment.

Remember that Mike entered therapy with many of the same symptoms and a similar history of troubled and disturbing behavior; his mother described him as defiant, unresponsive, constantly truant, uncooperative with any and all family rules, and smoking marijuana daily. But the psychotherapy took a very different course from Patrick's. I said very little, yet his behavior began to change substantially in only about 15 sessions.

Mike had agreed, for example, to call his mother when he wanted to stay out past his curfew, but he persistently "forgot". As result, his mother would become understandably incensed, there was greater friction in the house, he lost privileges, and in general his life was all the more miserable. A simple "Ma, I'm at Jim's; I'll be home an hour late if that's OK" would have allowed him to stay out and would have avoided all the hassle.

Why didn't I simply tell him this? Two reasons stand out among the many: First, Mike was more than smart enough to know already. Second, it wouldn't have worked. In all the talks about his behavior problems he'd already had with guidance counselors, school principals, relatives, and his parents, he had heard this many times. What magic would be accomplished by my repeating it? When someone is acting so counterproductively – when they fail to see the painfully obvious – unless they are simply dumb, the explanation for their behavior must lie in some other agenda than the current situation.

Mike and I didn't discuss that other agenda any more than we did his symptoms. I never pointed out how silly and self sabotaging he was being by his failure to call home; I never speculated on or suggested why he might be doing this (e.g. resenting authority, wanting to upset or irritate his parents, etc.); I never spoke about alternative ways to express his feelings or his rebellion or whatever was going on with this behavior. Yet Mike began to calm down and think clearly. His own natural and formidable intelligence came into play, and he found his own way back from being lost and stuck. He came in one day and reported some big changes.

One feature of his personality that had troubled many, including a school psychologist who tested him, was an apparent fantasy that he would always be able to "handle it", that things would always work out, despite the mounting evidence to the contrary – his ever deteriorating academic performance and interpersonal relationships. Suddenly Mike told me that he could see his attitude as "big talk; I just say it to convince myself". We were then able to discuss his genuine and quite opposite feeling of impending chaos and total failure.

At the same time, he started complying with the few rules and limits his family imposed on him, including the telephone calls home when he wanted to stay out late. He cut back on the marijuana and missed less school. He even told me how these behaviors were means of avoiding the great discomfort of his true feelings about himself and his life; he would cut school and avoid contact with his family in large part because dealing with school and family reminded him of how scared, inadequate, and out of control he felt. Yes, as always in psychology, the content of these discoveries sound common, obvious, even trite, but if I or a book or anyone else had tried to tell him it would have been useless. The therapy succeeds and a person changes because of his personal, emotional connection to the discoveries, because of insight.

With Mike, I did not address his behavior or his feelings until he did. I did not administer advice or in any other way try to talk him out of his behavior. I did not work with the family on their handling of discipline and rule-breaking. I did not try to alert him to the irrationality of his behavior, I did not suggest alternative behaviors, and did I not teach him "coping skills". I did not even try in any direct way to increase his awareness of his experiences, his feelings. In fact, I might be hard pressed to describe exactly what I did do. But you cannot argue with data, and the data are that after years of deteriorating behavior, this boy was turning his life around and feeling much better following only a few months of psychotherapy.

So what was the treatment? I provided a relationship, a space in which Mike could experience, remember, feel, and process. Sounds rather fuzzy, I know, but it worked. If I can't provide that place for Mike, nothing I say or do will have any impact on him; he will dismiss me and psychotherapy with the easy bravado that he uses everywhere. But if that relationship does happen, Mike will feel safe and free enough to consider alternatives to his usual way of thinking, feeling, acting, his usual *modus operandi*.

It was, for example, within the context of our relationship, with its safe, reflective, and yet light atmosphere, that Mike finally began to question his position that he "just forgets" to call his mother. (Of course, we already know he is resisting on this topic because of the "j" word.) He remembered that in the moment he actually does think of calling, but then immediately says to himself, "Nah, it'll be easier not to". This little piece of internal dialog was always edited out of awareness. Once he remembered it, he could see how silly and counterproductive it was and even why he was doing it. He recognized in it that habit of retreating into bravado when he is uncomfortable. Mike would be unlikely to make this discovery if he felt that discomfort in sessions with me. He has to trust me and the therapy at a level deep enough to allow such admissions of his true feelings and behavior. More than any specific thing I said or did, then, it was the relationship that did the healing (or more precisely, allowed healing to happen).

What Cures?

I never talked to Mike specifically about his irrationality, any more than I did with John, the psychotic patient I described at the beginning of this chapter. Telling John his perceptions were irrational, telling Mike that not calling his mother was irrational, would be just about futile. It only runs up against the patients' resistance. Mike would dismiss me as another authority trying to control him, John might politely nod but maintain his psychotic beliefs (or he might have become angry or even violent at my contradicting him).

Instead, what we do in psychotherapy is clear the way for the patient's own ego – his own intelligence, judgment, striving for mastery – to do its job. We clear away the resistance and defenses so that the patient can see for himself who he is and what he wants and needs. As one colleague put it, "my job is to help clean off people's glasses".

It works. I do not have to tell a patient what to do about his marriage, career, paranoia, anxiety, etc. If I can help the patient become more aware of his thoughts, actions, feelings, desires, needs, then he will know better than I what is best for him. Only when a patient truly cannot function do I have to be more directive, as with Patrick's mother, helping her to take a more consistent stance towards her son and to follow through on regaining control of the family.

Unfortunately, this feature of psychotherapy – clearing away the resistance so that a patient can discover the truth of his feelings, behavior, actions, perceptions – can make it seem like the therapist isn't doing anything. Mike's mother was angry with me during the entire course of his treatment for this reason; even when she saw the outcome, she remained resentful of my "ignoring" her son's problems.

Then when the insights came and Mike's behavior did change, it all seemed so obvious to her, as it always does to those of us outside the problem. There is little profound or complicated about Mike's failure to call home; anyone can see it as a misguided expression of his resentment, compensation for fear of rejection and/or humiliation, or just a clumsy attempt at being more independent. Few of us are really fooled by a teenager's "I just forgot" even if the speaker believes it. So why do you need an expert? Why psychotherapy?

During interviews, Scott McNealy, the former head of Sun Microsystems and now CEO of Wayin, was fond of responding "Duh!" to what he saw as the particularly obvious. I often hear that voice when I'm trying to explain anything about psychotherapy. If you look back at the examples of resistance from the previous chapter, an outsider would almost always have this reaction to the patient's insight and breakthrough. Patients themselves experience it.

My favorite example of this phenomenon occurred during my work with Barbara, a patient who suffered the loss of her best friend. This childhood friend, who later became her business partner, died suddenly of a long standing heart condition. Barbara called me about two weeks later, saying she had been in bed all day feeling on the verge of "losing it." During our conversation, she choked up and finally cried openly. Through her tears, she moaned about having an anxiety attack. "What's happening to me?" she wailed. What she had was grief over the loss of her friend coupled with some anxiety about losing long standing support. The feeling of panic came because she was being overwhelmed by feelings she feared and wanted to avoid. I said something like, "Of course you are crying and staying in bed all day, Barbara; your oldest and closest friend just died." Suddenly she laughed through her tears and said "I never thought of it like that. How stupid." We talked a bit more and she hung up feeling no happier but much saner. Barbara had this odd blind spot as part of a lifelong pattern of complete denial of the normal emotional reactions to stress, trauma, loss, etc. Even the most obvious of such reactions fell prey to her long standing need to rise above what she always felt was "weakness".

Patients sometimes come in having at last realized something about themselves that they never were able to see. In the telling, they find themselves feeling stupid, as Barbara did. They can hear that they are recounting the hopelessly obvious with great excitement to the very person who probably knew all along. Patients even apologize to me for it.

This phenomenon is so common that many branches of the profession have developed quips to describe it. In Alcoholics Anonymous it is said, "Denial ain't a river in Egypt." In other words, this kind of resistance is not just something you read about, not something you can know intellectually; when you see it in yourself – and therefore feel it – it's a powerful and highly personal experience. Some psychoanalysts like to say "Trite is right." That is, when you try to put your hard-won and liberating insights into words, they do tend to sound hopelessly obvious and vaguely icky. I think this is why psychology often sounds so asinine on talk shows. So when you find yourself expressing something you are sure you feel deeply yet it comes out sounding trivial, even sickeningly touchy-feely, you're probably on the right track.

Therapy vs. the Therapeutic.

In trying to understand what psychotherapy is, it would help to note what it isn't. While all the things I didn't do with Mike – help him analyze or evaluate his behavior, offer suggestions, help him and his family with discipline, limits, rules, help him develop alternate ways of coping – can be essential elements of a course of treatment, they are not psychotherapy. They are therapeutic, and might be termed "counseling". But in therapy, the relationship provides much more than the sum of the techniques used. And sometimes the treatment (and the relationship) must happen in the almost complete absence of these counseling techniques, as we saw with Mike.

The critical element then is not some specific kind of guidance, counseling, training, support, nor anything else the therapist has to offer, although these may be needed; rather it is the unique relationship that develops between a patient and a therapist. Another therapist might have handled Mike differently and gotten the same results. Meanwhile I might not be successful using that therapist's techniques, nor he using mine. (As one mentor told me, "you can't do someone else's shtick.")

This is not to say by any means that psychotherapy is an endlessly comforting, "warm fuzzy" experience. Quite the contrary. I was hardly comforting with Patrick or his mother. Particularly in the early stages, I was more the voice of doom. Psychotherapy is not a massage. It is not "unconditional positive regard", although sometimes that's part of it. There is nothing wrong with support and nurturing, but they are not, by themselves, psychotherapy. You need to feel you can trust your therapist, but it's not necessary that you always be comfortable. In fact, if your therapist's questions don't stir up a little discomfort, you may not be getting anywhere.

Nor is psychotherapy advice. The world's full of advice. Part of what brings you to treatment is that you've become lost in that advice and can't sort out who's to heed; the last thing you need is yet another voice to consider. The goal of treatment is for you to rediscover your own voice, your own priorities, and the courage and focus to act on them. Then the next time you won't get so confused. It's like that old aphorism: Give a man a fish, you feed him for a day; teach him to fish, and you feed him for life.

There is, of course, nothing wrong with support, nurturing, and unconditional acceptance, and even with occasional advice. They can be quite comforting and helpful. To that end, they are <u>therapeutic</u>. But they are not <u>psychotherapy</u>. This is an important distinction, particularly when it comes to evaluating your therapist and the work you are doing together. You want to learn to fish, not have to return each session for a feeding; therapeutic measures may only be giving you the latter while leaving you stagnant in learning to identify and take care of yourself.

We have seen that successful psychotherapy achieves that grander goal by increasing your awareness. Thus, a good way to think of the distinction between psychotherapy and something that is therapeutic is to ask, "does it foster insight?" Again, by "insight" I do not mean anything merely intellectual. Recall, by way of examples, the moments of insight experienced by Evan, "Bully", Sandra, and Ron, and the changes that followed – increased energy, clarity of thought and purpose, improved mood, and the abating of their symptoms. This is the kind of learning that should be happening during psychotherapy sessions.

There are times, of course, when the therapeutic measure is the only one that works. When a therapist advises a depressed person to take up running or to get up and moving by 9 A.M., if only to do the laundry, these are therapeutic measures that will hopefully spark an energy to counter the depression and decrease the symptoms. That was likewise the point of suggesting hospitalization for Patrick and guiding his mother in setting (and sticking to) limits and consequences. If this kind of advice is the only intervention, however, it's not psychotherapy; the person will learn nothing about his particular depression, what causes it, what sustains it, and what part of his personality is in pain. Instead, he may simply become a slave to activity in order to avoid depression. This is not a bad way to be, in principal, but such behaviors provide only limited coping skills for future disappointments; and every life has disappointment. As life progresses, particularly as age begins to be felt, it is very possible that this flight from depression will fail and depression will come crashing in again. You probably know people who seem to be bursting with energy most of the time and periodically sink into despair or isolate themselves to regroup. If this kind of depressed person can learn what makes him tick, what he fears, what he needs and how to get it, then he can identify these emotional issues when they rear up in the future; having those issues in awareness they are much less likely to take over his life again.

Types of Psychotherapy.

There are a very few kinds of psychotherapy that do not foster awareness: Behavior therapy is the main one. Behavioral treatments came out of laboratory work with animals and involve the principals of learning – positive and negative reinforcement, conditioned reflexes, and many others. Behaviorists have had success with certain kinds of patients and most therapists incorporate behavioral techniques into their work.

In behavioral treatments, a variety of exercises may be prescribed for the office and for the patient's life between sessions. These exercises hopefully eliminate symptoms in something like 10 to 30 sessions. They might involve gradual exposure to the thing you are afraid of, relaxation exercises to accompany this work (breathing, contracting and relaxing muscles, visualization, etc.), and various kinds of practice for the real life situation.

Behavioral treatment seems to work best on specific and circumscribed symptoms. By that I mean it can be useful if you really have no symptom other than your elevator phobia. As we saw in the first chapter, however, there are usually many other symptoms and even the phobia you think you have turns out not to be a phobia. It is best, therefore, to talk to the best therapist you can find – behavioral or otherwise – before you decide what kind of treatment you need.

What works for you will also change over time. I saw a man in his early twenties who asked about cognitive therapy. It would not have worked at the time. He was very adroit, intellectually and verbally, and he quickly skittered away from any of the insights offered by cognitive therapy, rapidly out-reasoned any suggestion, and had a variety of just barely conscious ways of distracting the session, changing the subject, evading any exploration of his life, of the very topics he brought into session. What he needed was a mix of supportive and at times quite confrontational work to break through all this resistance. Only later, when he could acknowledge just how insecure and evasive he was, and how intolerant of his own "weakness", could he open up to cognitive therapy and really question his deeply held and at times quite wild beliefs.

One problem with behavioral techniques is that they are inconsistently applied in real life, outside the session. This is especially the case when working with children and their families. It can be difficult for parents and schools, with their own styles and busy schedules, to really stick to the reinforcement schedules, limits, and consequences that are established in session. Still, properly applied, behavioral techniques can be very useful with some of children's specific problems such as tantrums, bed wetting, toilet training, and phobias.

As to distinctions among other forms of therapy currently in vogue, I would like to offer the scandalous assertion that it really makes little difference to you. Apart from behavior therapy, all successful courses of psychotherapy involve the kind of insight I have illustrated. Yes, there are differences in how one attains that insight, but the important difference is between good and bad therapists, not between schools of therapy. Research has shown this rather consistently. It turns out that successful vs. unsuccessful therapy is the distinguished by the quality of the therapist and of the relationship, not by the type of treatment.

By way of illustration, let's return to the case of Evan, the patient concerned with how marital separation would affect his relationship with his 5 year old son. Take a moment and review the insight he gained in session as described at the beginning of this chapter. Evan told me that he did not trust his wife to speak fairly about him to his son. I knew from our work together that much of his long buried feelings of self-doubt and inadequacy were tied up in his son. He was fiercely protective of the boy, easily reduced to tears at the thought of causing him any suffering, and had a series of recurring dreams in which his own and his son's identities were blurred and often merged. I also knew that this worry over his son somehow being brainwashed by his mother was unfounded for a number of reasons, including the boy's own statements indicating he was not blind to his mother's distortions and moments of irrationality.

At this juncture, I might have chosen among several approaches. I might have taken a cognitive focus and highlighted the irrational belief that his son would be so susceptible to suggestion; in a similar vein I might have focused on the irrational belief that he has no influence over or relationship with his son that could withstand a little bad-mouthing from mother. I might have taken a Freudian approach and suggested that his worry about his son's opinion of him reflected his feelings of inadequacy or competition in relation to his own father or to me. As an Interpersonalist (or what is now being called a Relational psychologist) I might have addressed these as well, although in different terms. As a Gestaltist I might have challenged his whining, challenged his lack of faith in his son, or dared him to explore just how bad he felt about himself. As a Jungian, I might have invoked the universal fears of separation and disintegration, or appealed to Evan's "shadow" and/or his "animus" to help him cope with the problem. As a reality therapist, I might have confronted his apparent fantasy that a divorce should not come with bumps and pain, that other fathers don't have to face the same problems and worse, and that he would not have to do a little work to maintain his good relationship with his son. And so on and on.

The lovely surprise is that any of these interventions might have proven successful, might have brought the increased awareness that we saw cleared the way for his change in attitude, feelings, and behavior. The best choice of these interventions depends on Evan's and my styles and personalities, and on our specific relationship. If you look again at that list of different things I might have said to Evan, they may appear different on the surface; underneath, however, you can see that they all will lead to Evan confronting his own insecurities as they are played out in his perceptions of his relationship with his son. As one colleague of mine put it "Good therapy is good therapy, only the babble is different". (Another, who had trained at a psychoanalytic institute reputed to be one of the best in the world, and who had subsequently pursued even more advanced training, put it even more succinctly: "They're all saying the same shit.")

What I did say to Evan's "I don't trust my wife" was, "It sounds like you don't trust your son". He was silent for a moment and then made a leap of his own. He sat up suddenly, his voice now much stronger, and said that what he really didn't trust was himself, and that this is why he had no belief that his son would maintain his good opinion of and relationship with Daddy. On the contrary, he realized, he believed his son would in a heartbeat forget about his "silly old, negligent, working class father" (Evan's words). He then went on to bring up an event of the previous week as a proof of this intense self-doubt. His wife had said "I need to talk to you" and he found himself "lying on the bed waiting in anxiety like I'm gonna face the school principal, wondering 'what did I do? what did I do'. Even after all this time of knowing just how out of line she is and how I really don't deserve to feel like this, I still get these waves of guilt and fear." This led to a discussion of dreams he usually brushed aside which had plagued him all his life; in them, he was always being similarly dismissed as trivial, by people who in life had no such attitude toward him.

Evan was then able to consider with a much clearer head the possibility of ending the marriage and the subsequent custody arrangements for his son. Here, as in the previous chapter's examples, we see the surge of energy, memory, insight, and confidence that are the typical reaction to a productive exchange between patient and therapist.

What counts is not the therapist's theoretical orientation or technique, but whether what he says clicks for you. Period. If it does not, all the theory, advice, counseling, training, credentials, and coaxing will not lead to any increase in your mastery of your emotional life or to any change in your feelings or behavior. What I chose to do with Evan was that which I felt would be accessible to him. I believe that many practitioners are similarly eclectic; they may have a theoretical orientation that is closest to their heart, they may call themselves analysts or cognitive-behaviorists, but they believe in aspects of many systems and they practice with a variety of techniques.

Freud is the father of it all, and like many fathers he is much maligned and misunderstood. When I was in college, I took two separate seminars which covered Freud. When I got to graduate school, I discovered that my professors had seriously misquoted and mislabeled him. If professors at Columbia University are misrepresenting Freud to their undergraduate students, surely the public who are not taking advanced psychology courses in such universities are hearing the same distortions or worse. In chapter 1 we saw some examples of how he's been mistranslated and his writing emasculated.

Turning to actual practice, when you find a therapist who claims to be a Freudian you unfortunately don't really know what you are getting. I've heard it said that if Freud were alive, he'd vigorously distance himself and his name from those calling themselves "Freudian". One thing to keep in mind is that a therapist who claims to be a "strict Freudian" is likely to have a rather rigid point of view about what made you the person you are, what your symptoms mean, and how to help you with them. This may work for you but if it does not, this therapist may not adjust his style to one that will.

If you are considering "Freudian analysis" bear in mind that psychoanalysis is a quite specialized form of treatment. It involves seeing the analyst 3-5 times a week and a commitment of probably 2 years and up; you will be on a couch during the sessions, the analyst probably sitting out of your range of vision. This treatment is not for everyone, but a good analyst will tell you if it is right for you within the first two or three sessions. Actually, most analysts I know do not start an analysis unless the patient has had at least a brief course of psychotherapy.

There are many other schools of psychoanalysis. They vary in theoretical orientation and in the structure of the sessions – the use of the couch, the number of sessions per week, content emphasized, etc. What they have in common is that treatment tends to last for at least a year, is usually at minimum twice per week, and the emphasis is on the past and the deeper layers of the personality.

When you hear about other kinds of specific psychotherapies such as "Cognitive therapy", "Dialectical Behavior Therapy", "Brief term psychodynamic therapy," "Cognitive-Behavioral Therapy," or variations on these names, remember two things. First, as I stated above, you will find that successful psychotherapy will cover the same issues in your life, whether the babble is about "irrational belief systems" (cognitive therapies) or "underlying feelings" (psychodynamic/psychoanalytic therapies). The important thing is that once the therapy gets under way, you should be hearing things that make sense to you, that intrigue you, and that ultimately lead to the kind of emotional revelation and change in mood and behavior that I have described.

Second, let me share with you what I learned about a lot of these kinds of psychotherapies as I studied them over the years. They have all contributed to my stock of therapeutic tools and techniques, and most have provided valuable food for thought and ways of thinking about patients. As therapies unto themselves, however, I noticed an interesting trend. They are often presented in a book written by the therapy's creator, and these books frequently follow the same pattern. The first half or so talks about the theoretic orientation behind the therapy, the impetus for its development – the author's dissatisfaction with other forms of therapy – and usually how widely applicable and remarkably successful the therapy is. The rest of the book gets into specifics of how to do the therapy, on whom it is most and least successful, and the results of research into the treatment. What emerges from this second half of these books is the fact that despite the claims of the first half, the treatment only works on a very limited and rather unidimensional kind of patient, one whom I have rarely seen – someone with, say, a phobia but no anxiety about anything else, with depression or obsessive symptoms but no anger or resistance to treatment.

So these treatments may seem compelling on first reading about them; they are great in theory and often sound quite plausible. In the real world, however, people with their resistance and full panoply of personality quirks are usually too complex for any of them to be used in isolation.

Choosing a Therapist.

If so many therapists have essentially the same goal and even employ similar approaches to practice despite their seemingly divergent theoretical orientations, how do you pick one? Actually, I already stated the most important answer to this question: You pick a therapist who says things that click for you. But that's not quite fair to the poor therapist who's meeting you for the first time. So when should things be clicking? And how do you find one who's likely to get around to saying things that click sooner rather than later?

There is a great tendency in some people to seek out an expert in whatever area they think is relevant – a quite reasonable hold-over from the world of medicine where it makes much more sense. I am wary of this in the realm of psychological issues for two reasons. First, as I have been saying, people enter treatment because they have become lost or stuck. They may not even know what their symptoms are much less their diagnoses, if they even warrant one; the problems are usually masked by the symptoms which may be defensive and serve resistance or may be direct expressions of pain, and much of the important feelings and behavior that need to be addressed lies outside of awareness and conscious control. In short, people usually don't know what's wrong with them. So how can they know what kind of treatment or expertise they need from the therapist – or if therapy is even the best option?

Second, since psychotherapy is so dependent on the relationship, on the practitioner's ability to create an atmosphere in which you can relax your resistance, it is not necessarily in your best interest to search for an expert on a particular problem. It is of course laudable that a therapist has conducted research or pursued more advanced training in some specific area, but if that therapist is not good at doing psychotherapy then no amount of course work or research or scholarly publication will change that. I've seen video recordings of sessions with some master writers, researchers, and theoreticians in the field which were astounding to behold; these experts were at times remarkably awkward and ineffective in conducting actual therapy. You feel as though you're watching someone trying to ski a steep and twisty mountain slope before learning how to make a basic turn. It may well be that doing psychotherapy requires a certain "raw material" in the practitioner, and that the best therapists may not be the best scholars, researchers, or self-promoters.

As to expertise in specific areas, think for a moment about what it really means in the case of psychotherapy to be an expert in, say, obsessions or panic. Does that mean you are not an expert in other kinds of feelings and behavior? As we've seen throughout this book, people suffer from very similar core problems – how can you be an expert in bullies and not understand the flinchers? We saw that Tom complained of phobias, "Bully" of panic and anger, George of memory problems, Evan and Ron of indecision in relationships, Mike (well, his mother) of defiance and drug abuse, and the flincher of loneliness and timidity; yet underneath, they all had similar anxieties. So do you really want someone who appears to specialize in phobias, relationships, substance abuse, family therapy, bullying, or social anxiety?

Still, you have to start somewhere. How do you choose? Start with credentials. I mentioned in the last chapter that people often seem oddly uninterested in a therapist's credentials. I described this as a kind of resistance. Make the effort to conquer this, despite the discomfort it may cause, and ask.

Here is an important piece of information about credentials that is often overlooked. The term "psychotherapist" is unlicensed; anyone can call themselves a psychotherapist (or "therapist"). The terms "psychologist", "psychiatrist", and "licensed clinical social worker (LCSW)", "licensed master social worker (LMSW)", and some others, require some kind of licensure. The practitioner cannot use these titles without having met certain state and national requirements. Below are brief descriptions of these licensed practitioners, in descending order of what fees they usually charge. I'm writing from New York, where I practice; the requirements may vary somewhat in other states and they change. Consider the material below approximate when it comes to the social workers.

Psychiatrist: some kind of undergraduate pre-med degree, graduation from medical school, and then graduation from a psychiatric residency program. As medical doctors, psychiatrists are the only practitioners discussed here who can prescribe medication. There are rumblings in the field of certifying psychologists to do so, but don't hold your breath; it was going on 30 years ago when I was in school. Many psychiatrists are also "board certified", which requires them to take another competency exam after they are in practice. But bear in mind that unless the residency specifically focuses on psychotherapy, a licensed psychiatrist can conceivably have no training or experience in it! Most who practice psychotherapy do pursue advanced training; don't hesitate to ask about this. One problem, though, is that such advanced training usually takes place at a psychoanalytic institute. See "Psychoanalyst", below, for the danger here.

Psychoanalyst: A psychoanalyst must complete psychoanalytic training at an analytic institute. Sounds very advanced but there are some cautions. First, there are institutes and there are institutes. Second, some institutes accept candidates for training with little or no prior background in the field. At another extreme are institutes will not even consider an applicant other than a medical doctor who, as discussed above, may have no background in psychology or psychotherapy. A psychoanalyst, therefore, may be trained in only his analytic institute's possibly narrow view of the field. On the other hand, there are some institutes that I believe consistently produce the most competent and effective therapists.

Psychologist: a Ph.D. or a Psy.D. (a Ph.D. without the science emphasis) in psychology, requiring about 5 years of graduate training in psychology. Graduate clinical psychology students spend up to half their time in clinical settings – mental health centers, psychiatric hospitals, schools, clinics – and they receive one-on-one supervision of their work. There is also at least a year of full time internship in a clinical setting. In order to sit for the psychology licensing examination, most states require 1 or 2 years of post-graduate supervised experience in the field. (Make sure that your psychologist is a <u>clinical</u> psychologist. A psychologist who studied rats in graduate school can sit for the licensing exam, call himself a psychologist, and set up a practice, although I've never heard of one who did.)

Social Worker LCSW-R: An LCSW with three years (full time) of supervised psychotherapy work.

Social Worker, LCSW: Usually 2 years of graduate training with an emphasis on psychotherapy, an internship also emphasizing psychotherapy, and about half a year (full time) of supervised post-graduate work before obtaining the license.

Social Worker, LMSW: Master's degree in social work, which may or may not involve any training in psychotherapy or even human behavior, followed by half a year (full time) of supervised clinical experience.

Licensed Mental Health Counselor: Master's degree, internship, and two to three years of post-graduate supervised clinical experience.

My own advice is that you choose well trained and widely experienced therapists. My reason is that among the most common errors made by therapists of limited training and experience is that of overlooking alternative explanations, diagnoses, and treatments. You would not want to be seeing a narrowly trained, narrowly focused therapist about depression if in truth you were suffering nutritional deficits, sleep deprivation, neurologic damage, chronic anxiety, or borderline personality, all of which can mimic depression. I see this danger most commonly in the case of Attention Deficit Disorder. Very often what looks like this disorder is any number of other conditions, including separation anxiety or interpersonal conflict among family and teachers. Before rushing to the Ritalin or Adderall (commonly prescribed medications for ADD), the condition should be carefully diagnosed and all alternative possibilities ruled out.

How do you find such a therapist? If you know people who have been or are in psychotherapy, and they are having success, you might ask to see their therapist. If this is a spouse or close family member, you probably shouldn't see the same therapist, but you can get names of other therapists that way. If you have a family doctor you trust, or an attorney or teacher, they might know good therapists.

You might also contact the health or guidance office of a school or company you are affiliated with and see who they recommend. Bear in mind, however, that these days many of these departments have contracted with managed care companies, Employee Assistance Programs, and other "preferred provider lists". If so, you are not getting a personal recommendation; you are getting names of therapists who have agreed to be on those lists, usually because they are willing to accept imposed fee structure and other contractual restrictions. There is nothing in this to encourage confidence that you are getting a good therapist.

A better route is to contact an analytic institute and apply for treatment. Training institutes sometimes run outpatient clinics where you can go for psychotherapy often at reduced rates. You might also apply to be seen for more intensive work by one of their trainees. These clinicians are studying at the institute and will be receiving supervision on your case. You will thus have the benefit of your therapist's eye and that of the therapist's more senior, supervising therapist.

Community mental health centers often offer sliding scale rates (i.e. based on your capacity to pay). Here you're taking luck of the draw, as you likewise are with telephone book. Look under "psychologist", "psychotherapy", "counseling", "mental health", etc. Remember that any advertisements you see in the yellow pages or newspapers are efforts to solicit business. They should be read with the same skepticism you would apply to any advertising. In any of these cases you could get the best help there is, the worst, or anything in between. I know someone who simply called the first licensed psychologist she found in the telephone book that was within an hour of her home; she ended up with someone well respected by his peers and he has been of tremendous help to her.

You can also try your insurance company. If you are in one of the managed care health insurance programs, and who of us isn't these days, you will want to see an "in network provider" or "preferred provider" – someone with whom the insurance company has a contract to see patients. Your "co-payment" – the portion of the fee that is not covered and which you will have to pay – will be low, usually between about 10 and 60 dollars per session. Unfortunately, now you are really taking pot luck. First, you don't know how these companies choose their providers. Second, it is to these companies' financial advantage to send you to a social worker rather than a psychologist or psychiatrist because they pay social workers a lower rate per session; if you want a psychologist or psychiatrist, you may have to insist. Third, most of the clinicians I admire have quit the managed care panels; there are hopefully good clinicians still there, but you may have to dig.

Something else to keep in mind is that managed care companies are not motivated to authorize sessions for you. One company used to insist after only about 12 sessions that I send my patients to a psychiatrist for medication. (I have quit that company's provider list.) In any event, be prepared eventually to pay your therapist out of your own pocket once insurance stops authorizing sessions. In fact, even with "out of network benefits", wherein you can see a therapist of your choice for the plan's maximum number of visits per year, some companies refuse to reimburse for such out of network sessions if you see the <u>same</u> in-network therapist after authorization runs out. If you want your sessions covered according to whatever out of network benefits you have, you might then have to change therapists. Finally, be aware that in order to have sessions authorized, your therapist may have to discuss your case in detail with "case managers" at the managed care companies; this data will be entered into computer files. It is rare, but there are cases if people having difficulty getting disability insurance because they had records of claims for psychotherapy.

After credentials, what should you consider? Talk to your new therapist. Even in a first telephone contact you can get a feel for him: Does the therapist have patients similar to how you describe yourself? Most important, do you feel a sense of comfort from and confidence in the person you are talking to? If not, call someone else. There is no point in seeing a therapist who leaves you cold. You must trust your own response to the therapist, hard as that may be. Then, as therapy progresses, try to keep in mind what I've said about data and logic. You should be able to understand why the therapist believes what he does about you, how he arrived at his opinions, even if it is at first hard to agree.

A word about that first telephone contact and about "failed" therapy. Psychotherapy is a relationship and few relationships proceed without bumps; give it a fair try. No-one in any relationship says the perfectly right thing all the time. But if you keep your eyes open – we will discuss how to do that below – there is no reason for failure to mean anything more than minimal lost time and money. This is not brain surgery where one wrong move leaves you paralyzed. If you meet with a therapist for a few sessions and it is not working, you have lost little and you will doubtless have learned at least something from the experience, if only more precisely what you want in a therapist. If you've stayed longer, and you have kept your eyes open, you should have learned something and maybe even changed a bit. I described such a case in the previous chapter. Sara, you recall, made good progress for over a year, but then developed an intense resistance to me and chose to leave treatment. Her departure was unfortunate, not as we would wish, but in no way negates the progress she made before she left.

(I've often had the same thought about marriages. Children naturally leave the nest, students outgrow their teachers, but we expect a relationship formed at the age of 20 or 30 to sustain us decades later. People often refer to a marriage as "failed" because it ends. Is it "failure" that either or both of the parties continue to grow and change, perhaps at the expense of the marriage? It seems to me that a couple can love, share, grow, give to each other, learn from each other, and then grow apart and separate.

The fact of its ending should not invalidate the entire marriage. No, I am not divorced.)

Finally, it has always seemed curious that someone would object to a therapist because that therapist has had to struggle through his own craziness. Why <u>wouldn't</u> you want such a therapist? Isn't it more likely that someone who has had to come to grips with his own unconscious – uncover his own lies, find his own way back from lost and stuck – would be better able to help you with yours, as compared with someone whose defenses have never failed him, who was perhaps able to stay blissfully unaware of any turmoil or confusion? How could such a lucky person help you find your way out of the mess? How could he help you navigate your own conflicting, confusing, and half-buried feelings, through all the roadblocks your resistance will throw in the way, with little or no personal experience of such amorphous, intangible, and even counterintuitive phenomena? (I wonder if that's what goes wrong with the therapy sessions conducted by the kind of academic masters I described above – if perhaps they are missing the personal experience that enables them to connect to a patient in turmoil.)

Think for a moment about learning a sport. The natural, who never had to work at it, may have no idea why your golf swing isn't working. I remember taking a tennis lesson with a wonderful player who kept saying "do it like this"; I did, but it never worked and he was unable to suggest just how I could fix my swing. The born klutz, on the other hand, has had to build up his skills step by step, carefully identifying and unlearning his own bad habits. He's the one I'd want diagnosing my swing. He is the one who can turn a practiced eye on my form and pick out the small burst of tension in my shoulder or slight last-second twist of my forearm that is causing the problem. The only thing you don't want is a therapist who is still acting out his problems, one whose feelings and behavior are out of control. We'll discuss how to spot such a creature in subsequent sections.

What Should Happen in a Session?

This is tricky. Relationships, even psychotherapeutic ones, do not follow rigid guidelines. Of course, if you are miserable in the first session, find someone else (unless you are miserable everywhere). Barring that, you and your therapist should agree on some time frame at which point you will discuss whether or not there has been any progress and in general how things are going. If a patient is comfortable with me in the first session and wants to return, I tell him to come 5 times. By then, I tell him, we should have a good idea what we will be discussing and how these discussions will proceed. He should have a sense of what a session feels like and what will happen, and should feel that the conversations are different from what he experiences elsewhere. It is important during this trial period to stick to the 5 sessions and not give in to obsessing over whether it's working, do you really like the therapist, can the therapist help, maybe you should have seen a woman, maybe you should have seen a man, etc. It's too early to know. It's like going to the gym twice and then checking to see if your muscles are getting bigger. You have to go for that first month, as you decided, and then you can stop and consider whether it's going anywhere.

Following this 5 session introduction, if things feel like they could move I tell patients that after another 10 sessions, maximum, they should see some change. Probably nothing dramatic, but some difference in how they think, feel, and act, or in how things look to them. That has become a rather conservative estimate. In fact, patients usually see some change sooner, sometimes pronounced change.

Sessions should be intriguing, engaging, at times uncomfortable. They may be erratic, inconsistent, and fraught with resistance that makes you want to quit, but there should be some overall sense of the new and interesting happening. You want to find yourself getting curious about what is making you think, feel, and act the way you do and how various aspects and events of your life are related in ways you hadn't considered.

You also want to feel that you are getting just a little closer to the truth of what you feel, what you do, and what you believe. If you walk out of all of those first five sessions with no sense of this and you're running out of things to say, bring it up with the therapist. It may be that your resistance is too great for psychotherapy at this point; it may be that this particular therapist in some way puts you on edge and you can't open up; it may be that you feel no connection to the therapist or for some other reason can't get interested in the process; it may be that therapy isn't right for you at that point. In any event, bring it up. If you feel no glimmer of resolution of this issue and things don't soon change, quit or find another therapist.

Once again, please note that you do not have to talk about your past, and you don't have to blame your mother for everything. One woman saw me for over 2 years, made a lot of progress, became quite a different woman in many ways, and yet we rarely discussed her past. Despite my personal belief in the importance of her childhood experiences, we were rarely able to explore the subject; when I tried, she would become impatient, at times hostile. Ultimately, she was right; it was not necessary to delve into her past at that point.

When we do talk about your mother, the goal is not at all to cast blame. If I point out to the bully that in his experiences with his mother it sounds like he felt intimidated, humiliated, powerless, and very anxious, my goal is to help him understand what he has lived through and what he continues to suffer and enact in current life; it really doesn't matter whether his mother was doing the best she could and was simply sloppy, or was a vicious sadist, or was entirely proper but the patient is hopelessly needy. What is salient is the intrusion of the bully's early experiences into his current life. The goal is to understand what happened to him, what effect it had, and how he continues to reenact it in the ongoing troublesome behaviors and feelings that have driven him to seek treatment.

Once your sessions are under way, it becomes too personal for me to tell you what will happen. One person's symptom that abates in 15 sessions is another's resistance that doesn't even surface until session 20.

Early in our work Ron, from chapter 4, admitted to me as he did to no one else the depths of his feelings of fragility, fear, and loneliness. After about a year of this, however, it became clear to both of us that he was now using these admissions as resistance. He was dwelling on these as a distraction from angry, bitter, vengeful, and even sadistic aspects of his personality. He was stuck in the experience of himself as a hurt, lost soul – something that a year earlier was a revelation to him. Meanwhile his less conscious feelings and acts of hostility were endangering his career and his personal life.

By contrast, Nancy spent the first six months of treatment relating to me as if I was a rival for a man's affection. She was sure I was trying to cheat her out of session time and she told me only the stories in which she felt either anger or the satisfaction of having gotten her way. It was only after half a year with me that she began to drop this resistance and acknowledge how uncertain and lost she really felt. Her deepest feelings were Ron's means of resistance, and vice versa. Your own road from lost and stuck to awareness and freedom will be unique to you.

Time Frame and When to Stop.

Sorry, but there is no easy answer here either. In my experience gross anxiety symptoms clear up rather quickly, sometimes in under 10 sessions, usually by session 25 or so. This applies to phobias, panic attacks, some obsessions and compulsions, and some social anxieties. If there is no progress in these areas after a few months, it is time to consider other treatments including behavior therapy, biofeedback, or medication, if they haven't already been tried. Also, if these symptoms have progressed to the point that you cannot function, then you really have little choice other than medication.

Other kinds of symptoms can take much longer to abate. In general, symptoms which are less circumscribed take longer. In other words, if the symptoms are part of generalized patterns of troublesome behavior and feelings in your life, they are not going to evaporate as quickly. This should make some intuitive sense. A behavior that is more embedded in your personality, in your overall way of getting through life, will be more difficult to uproot than one that feels like a thorn in your otherwise comfortable side.

It can take a long time, however, just to tell your story in therapy, even if you feel highly motivated to do so. Especially if you've never really told the whole truth to someone – and this is more common than we like to admit – it can be hard to let another person know your secrets. Meanwhile, it may appear to those outside the session that not much is happening. I think that's unfair to patient and therapist. Someone with this resistance may be honestly trying to talk, but old habits die hard and lies are hard to give up. Many people consciously and in good faith try to tell their therapist what hurts, but the stories come out confused, incomplete, censored, sanitized.

Once a person does begin to talk openly, he may find that the one thorn which brought him into treatment is part of a whole thorny branch. The symptom may be the most noticeable, most disturbing expression of a; and that problem could well be causing a myriad of less obvious symptoms – perhaps which the person resists seeing but which are none-the-less fouling up his life. We saw that in the case of Greg who steadfastly denied that he felt or expressed any hostility towards his son; we saw it in Bully who said he was fine until he started getting "restless" a few years before contacting me.

Remember that Tom (chapter 2) came in complaining of anxiety symptoms but then, as he spoke about the interpersonal confrontations that seemed to trigger his anxiety, began noticing other problems. He described being "high strung and perfectionistic" on his job. If one of his employees was doing something quite menial which he felt could be done better he would rush in and take over the work. He knew enough not to fire the employee on the spot – that is, he knew that it was his perfectionism and not the employee's failing that was the cause of his tension – but he could not control the feeling beyond that. He began describing similar tension at home. As we discussed all of this, the phobias began to abate. Within a mere 15 sessions, he was reporting no phobic symptoms and they did not recur. He was, however, discussing a range of interpersonal situations that caused him great tension and often rage. As we talked about them, we began to discuss his past in more detail, including his childhood.

With Tom, the problems that led him to seek treatment sat atop deeper problems which affected many areas of his life. Those top-level symptoms dissipated rather quickly but by then he had become invested in working on the more insidious and deeply ensconced patterns of behavior and feelings that were interfering with his functioning and happiness. We then worked on rooting out the malfunctioning branches of his personality in contrast with his original focus on the few thorns that peaked out from under his resistance and got his attention.

It turned out that much of Tom's distressing and apparently unjustified feelings of panic, rage, impending catastrophe, powerlessness centered on a story from his childhood. When he somewhat abruptly and with little obvious reason blurted this story out, adding that "I've always remembered this for some reason", the therapy took off. He began acknowledging more and more of his discomfort, instead of sitting in my office in palpable distress yet shrugging everything off. So much of his discomfort finally made sense to him, as reenactments of that childhood experience.

To an outsider, and indeed to Tom, this can all sound rather fantastic; he was given to punctuating our discussions with "I can't believe how this stuff works." But the change in his functioning, the easing of his anxieties and the improvement in his relationships with family, friends, and coworkers, was quite real. He described ever increasing calm with others, greater power and confidence in his handling of business and interpersonal problems, and a widening range of activities. In sessions, when he made the connection from the present to this story from the past, he would become much calmer, more optimistic.

Let's pause a moment to notice some features of Tom's case that illustrate points I have made in this book. 1) Psychotherapy does not necessarily address symptoms directly. Tom's symptoms are irrational in that nothing in his current life can account for such feelings and behavior (panic, rage, phobic avoidance). Yet those symptoms evaporate fairly quickly as we start attending to the rest of his life. 2) Isolation; 3) screen memories, discussed later in this chapter. Tom remembers an event vividly but without much emotion beyond curiosity as to why the event has stayed with him. 4) What we don't feel/remember, we are doomed to act out. 5) Logic and data drive the therapy into whatever territory eventually reaches. Much of Tom's disturbing feelings and behavior are rational and even necessary when viewed as reactions to his childhood experiences. 6) The patient's reaction is the measure of whether we are on the right track. That we are onto something real and not just engaging in speculation or psychobabble is shown by Tom's reaction of increased calm, clarity, and optimism. Finally, 7) increasing awareness leads to desired changes in feelings, attitude, and behavior. As Tom explored this dynamic in his life, how it played out in so many diverse situations, he remembered more of the affect in that original childhood experience; at the same time, his functioning in daily life improved and his disturbing feelings and behavior abated.

In contrast with Tom's treatment, there are situations where there is little or no improvement visible to the outside world even in several months of sessions. This does not mean nothing is happening. Some patients take longer to open up to the treatment. People are ready at different times in their lives to let another person, even their own therapist, get to know them. While they keep the therapist at arm's length, they may tell only partial stories about themselves and may withhold other stories entirely. We saw this in the examples of Nancy and Ron, contrasted in the previous section. This resistance is often part of a general anxiety state that is so habitual that it's hardly noticed by the patient. It feels natural, even comfortable and familiar. Yet it prevents them from thinking clearly and answering a simple question like "And what did you do then?" without a great deal of censoring, confusion, and withholding. This is especially common with children and adolescents, but it happens with adults as well. It even occurs with patients who on the surface are eager to start the process. Tom used to struggle to follow our discussion and would complain "I'm trying but I get all mixed up." This was the resistance of confusion and it was unconscious; at a conscious level, he was trying his best.

Joe, age 53, used this defense with particular tenacity. He would balk, get lost in irrelevant detail, drift off in his attention, hesitate and stall in getting to the point, leave sentences unfinished, and so on. The more I inquired for clarity in his stories, the more murky it all became. Gradually during treatment he was able to see these patterns in his speech and identify them as resistance. Once we finally got some complete stories he began to see that he had been (unconsciously) sanitizing his reporting, censoring out data. He would tell me, for example, of a family gathering in which there was conflict, but he would leave out his own nasty comments. When he was able to notice the signs of this happening – the halting speech, the wandering attention, the confusion – he slowly began telling more complete stories, including in them his own unflattering behavior and eventually his confused and upsetting emotional reactions.

Joe and I worked a fairly long time just to get him to this point of telling his doctor what hurts. Meanwhile, it may have appeared on the outside that he was having months of psychotherapy to no avail. He simply was not ready to begin the process any sooner. He needed those months of getting comfortable with me, while I repeatedly brought the blocks in his speech to his attention, before he could begin speaking openly.

Once the symptoms that brought you into treatment have eased a bit, then what? Psychotherapy can be a long term process, like any education. There are almost always more unsatisfying feelings and behavior to explore, more layers of resistance and defense to conquer, more of the self to bring into consciousness and master, i.e. more lies to expose. So when is enough enough? When do you stop?

The answer is: When you want to.

Chris, age 31, came to see me in a state of great anxiety, mostly concerning his relationship with his mother and how it was affecting his marriage and other relationships. He felt he could not even talk to his mother on the telephone, he worried that he was going crazy, and he wanted to see me 2 or 3 times a week. Early in treatment, he learned how to handle his mother's very subtle brand of control and denigration, how to take a position with her and stick to it, and how to avoid raging at his wife when he felt cornered by his mother. We also began to explore similar problems in his other relationships – with his wife, father, brother, colleagues, bosses, etc. He was most troubled by a constant feeling that he was about to be blamed for something and by his angry, intolerant outbursts towards his wife, father, and brother. As he became more aware of exactly what he was feeling at these moments – anger was the tip of the iceberg – and of where those feelings actually originated (it was not where he thought), there were changes. His anxiety eased, his interactions became more appropriate, he was less paranoid at work and with his wife, and he felt more confident and centered.

After about 5 months of weekly sessions, Chris felt strong and independent enough to cut his visits back to alternate weeks. Progress continued for another few months to the point where he was ready to open up an old photo album he had come across during a recent cleaning of his attic. When he began to look at the album, he told me, tears welled up and he quickly put it away. This impulse to cry began to arise at other, relatively mild stimuli – a song on the car radio, the sight of his children playing. He was reluctant to explore this newly discovered wellspring of emotion. He found it "scary" and was quick to distract himself when it arose.

Soon thereafter, Chris came in and said he'd made a decision. He was not going to open the photo album just yet, nor would he let the tears well up at other times. He said he was not ready for whatever might emerge if he allowed the tears. He was grateful for the work we had done, but he wanted to stop. He told me this.

> "It's like a favorite birthday present that you want to postpone opening. It's like a security blanket – I know that the album is there for me if I start feeling out of touch or crazy or anxious again. Or if I start getting really uptight around people, or yelling at my wife. I know if I look at it and let the feelings and memories happen, things will make sense again. Painful as it may be, I'll end up saner. But for right now, I want to keep it put away – the album and my memories or feelings or whatever."

This is a good reason to stop. You've made the progress you wanted and don't want to go further.

The only caution here is that sometimes the desire to stop comes out of resistance, and resistance should not be indulged without a fight. Remember, resistance can block you from what you actually want, from doing and saying and believing what is most true of you and what is in your best interest. The thing to do, then, is to talk about your desire to stop with your therapist. You should be able to agree on the progress you have made up to that point, the changes that have occurred, and where you stand currently. If you are satisfied with the latter, or if it is as far as you can go at that point in time, it may indeed be best to stop treatment. One clue to this situation is a period of stagnation in treatment but in the absence any hint of brittle, tense resistance.

Resistance tends to express itself in fairly strong and unpleasant emotions. For example, if you find yourself furious with your therapist, suddenly bored with him, if you can't seem to remember why you ever liked him in the first place, if you can't remember what you got out of treatment, these are signs that resistance is at play (assuming of course that you did previously find your therapist useful). What such irrational emotion means is that the therapy is beginning to stir up something in you that you are struggling to avoid. If you can get to it, therapy will take a substantial jump forward. If you cannot, again it is time to stop. Even in the worst case of this kind, when you are thoroughly and unreasonably disgusted with your therapist, you can agree that no progress is being made; you can agree that it is time at least for a hiatus. Sara in the previous chapter is an example of this situation. She had made some big changes in her life during out work together, conquering an intense self-consciousness around men that used to leave her endlessly obsessing over every casual encounter, she had learned a great deal about her other anxieties, and she had begun to break some self-destructive habits with her family. Prior to treatment, she let them put her down constantly, hardly recognizing it was happening after all these years yet walking around in a constant state of unwarranted self-denigration.

But unlike Tom, Sara could take these insights and new repertoire of behaviors only so far. She was for some reason too wedded to and comfortable with her old ways. In accordance with these old ways, she was unable to assert herself directly and simply terminate therapy without rancor, as Chris was able to do. Instead, as we saw, Sara had to make an enemy of me. She became unshakable in her perception that I was constantly criticizing and censoring her. Despite all my efforts to discuss this, and despite her own belief other times that I was not such an ogre, she could not see beyond this feeling. This had happened before, but never to this degree. It intensified over a period of several months, until we both agreed that at least for the present time there was nothing to be gained by our continuing. (Yes, those of you who know your psychodynamics are correct in thinking Sara had transferred onto me the rejection, judgment, and intolerance she'd felt from her family.)

Notice that it does not matter to you, the patient considering termination of treatment, which of us is right. It does not matter if Sara was, as I believe, reenacting her family relationships with me, blaming me for the rejection and negativity she experienced at their hands. It does not matter that, in my opinion, she will need to become conscious of that reenactment, of the distortions she brings to her relationships, in order to really be comfortable with anyone and to really shed the burden of unnecessary anxiety. These things don't matter because I was unable to communicate them in a way that reached Sara. I could not find a way to overcome her particular resistance. Her distrust of me therefore persisted and eventually she left treatment. And of course if I was completely wrong in my interpretation, if Sara's feelings of distrust of and persecution by me were in some way based in the reality of how I treated her, the result is still the same; time to stop seeing me.

A final word about Sara and when to stop therapy. Despite the unsatisfactory ending, her treatment was in no way a failure. She made clear and important gains in her anxiety level and her interpersonal relationships, as was her goal in the first place; she just didn't go as far as she could. The treatment was therefore productive even though it ended as it did; it does not matter whose point of view was accurate – mine that she was resisting or Sara's that I was a condescending critic. Once again, the bottom line: You should quit psychotherapy when you cannot make any further progress, regardless of whose fault it is.

There are a few times when there is little or no doubt that you should change therapists. In general, it is time to move on when you cannot talk about something. Your therapist's office is the one place where you must be free to talk about anything. In fact, part of your therapist's job is to help you talk about the difficult subjects you don't want to discuss. So if you have some discomfort or gripe with your therapist, it may be hard but you must bring it up. The two of you should be able to reach some resolution and understanding. Of course, you have to make a real effort to raise the issue and then to give your therapist a fair hearing; but if you do and you cannot find renewed confidence in the process, or at least faith that such confidence will resurface soon, it is time to find another therapist.

Also as a general rule, I think you should be wary of therapists who give advice, particularly early in treatment. As I said before, part of the reason you come to therapy is that you've become lost in all the advice available in the world and can't sort out which advice is best for you. Perhaps the last thing you need is yet another point of view to consider. The only exception to this is the case where you are simply not functioning, as we saw earlier in this chapter with Patrick. There are times when you may want your therapist's opinion, but that opinion should be on matters of psychology where his presumed expertise lies. If a therapist tells you that saying "Maybe I hate my wife/husband/parent/child" is an intellectual game, that it is more resistance than substance, I think you can listen to it. Similarly, if he tells you that your attachment to your current lover sounds to him like it is based on your love of escapism and not of that person, and thus to stop and think before you move in together, that sounds like fair game to me as well. But no therapist should be telling you flat out who to date or marry. What you want is for your therapist to help you consider your own rationale for those choices, to get you interested in your process, in sorting out your hidden agendas and motives in those decisions, i.e. in where you're not telling the truth. If you want your life to be based on your own needs, desires, and ultimately your own choices, you want a therapist who helps you find those in yourself, not one who imposes his.

On the more obvious front, if your therapist wants you to have sex with him (or her), if your therapist wants to borrow money from you, if he wants to be part of your business project, don't stop and think; just get out. You do not need to have a beer with your therapist, visit his country house, go to the opera with him, or hear about his personal life. The only time the latter would be appropriate is if he is telling about himself to help you understand your own life.

Finally, I think you should flee any therapist who says "You are resisting" when you disagree with or fail to understand him, but goes no further. If he cannot help you to see how that resistance is happening, why it is resistance and not some valid difference of opinion, then he is probably useless to you, even if he's right.

Screen Memories.

Take a look back at the discussion of Tom, in the previous section. Tom found that he could make sense of much of his perplexing, disturbing behavior and feelings by referring back to a single memory from childhood. When he was about 7 years old at the family's weekend house in the country, he and his friends did something wrong – he doesn't recall what but believes it was minor. His father reacted oddly. First he was disgusted; in Tom's memory the man's face was red and he looked as if he were about to hit Tom. Then in an almost smug tone told the boy his punishment would come after dinner that evening. Tom stewed all day over this, increasingly fearful and obsessed. In his room shortly after dinner his mother called for him to come to the top of the stairs so she could ask or tell him something. He vividly recalls the view of his room, his immobility and confusion – although interestingly not fear – as his mother called out to him with increasing impatience; he vaguely recalled a queasy dread that this second parent was now disgusted with him as father already was. This memory always stayed with Tom, popping up at odd times in his daily life for no apparent reason – as it did during one of our early sessions. He could not recall thinking or feeling much, either when it happened or in later recollecting it; he remembered only the sight of the room, the sound of his mother's voice, and being unable to take any action.

Sure enough, what we don't remember we are doomed to enact. The forgotten feelings from this story were evident in every troubling incident that Tom brought into session. For the first time he understood his overreactions – rage, paralyzing anxiety, abandonment, isolation, and so on. These feelings were always far too intense to be caused by current circumstances, but they made complete sense in the case of a 7 year old in the situation Tom recalled. The same applies to his behavior; when he rushed in with rage and disgust to take over the less-than-perfect (but more-than-adequate) work of an employee, he was 1) reenacting what was done to him when he was less than perfect at home and 2) trying to master or undo that original experience of impotence and indecision.

Once again, how do we know all of this is not mere speculation on my part, an interesting psychological construct which may have no relevance to Tom's real problems? All together now: Data! First, Tom had always remembered this story, as clearly as the day it happened. Why would that be unless there is some forgotten emotional import attached to it. Second, once he began speaking about this memory, he frequently found it relevant; it would jump into his head as we explored whatever event he had brought up in session. Third, and most important, whenever he made that connection from the present to the past, he felt clearer, more relaxed, more optimistic, and he functioned better. His symptoms finally made sense to him and abated once he saw them as reenactments of that childhood experience.

This kind of story, so vividly recalled and so relevant and central to all that goes on in Tom's life, has been called a <u>screen memory</u>. A screen memory is a story from the past that seems to encapsulate much, if not all, of a person's experience of himself and the world. It has become an unconscious lens through which all subsequent experiences are distorted.

In Tom's screen memory, he is helpless, lost, and alone, useless and disgusting to his parents. Don't forget that to a seven year old, parents are just about the whole world. So now in the reenactment, the world around him (especially his father) is always about to collapse disastrously (reject him in disgust) if he does not remain in complete control of everything including himself. This need for total control, incidentally, may also account for the panic attacks; such attacks usually involve the fear of losing control. We can see at least two important reasons for Tom's habit of rushing in angrily to take over his employees' trivial tasks. First, anything he is involved with must be handled perfectly; second, by taking over from an inadequate employee Tom finds comfort in playing his father's role in the screen memory, in being a chip off the old block. You may recognize in these reasons the basic pattern of defenses discussed in earlier chapters – doing what we had to in order to survive, and doing what was done to us.

Note that the accuracy of the screen memory is not at issue here. It may or may not be entirely true. Most often it is one story among many similar others; for whatever reason, it is the one that became most potent. It can also be an amalgam of several real events distilled into a single memory. But it does not matter. Whether the story is an exact retelling of the event as a camera would have seen, a partial view from the patient's memory, or an unconscious reconstruction of several similar situations, the fact is that this is how the patient experiences himself and the world.

Screen memories are self-reinforcing; they feed themselves in a vicious cycle. As we saw so clearly in the last chapter, people actively (but unconsciously) lie, rewriting history in accordance with their particular distortions, needs, experiences. Phil, in the previous chapter, was sure he had been ignored and rejected by a colleague who in fact did no such thing to him. By this editing process, his view of himself as the rejected, lost soul he was as a child, is reinforced. So not only is the memory reexperienced in current life, as in Tom's intense reactions of rage and panic to relatively mild stresses, but the data of current life are rewritten to conform to the memory; in this way the memory is strengthened as a relevant, dominant, and even accurate view of life.

Not every patient I work with comes out with a screen memory. You need not feel that treatment is doomed without one; many successful treatments pass without it. But it happens often and when it does, psychotherapy is particularly exciting for both patient and therapist.

(You can see another example of how screen memories operate in "Bully", the second case example in chapter 1. In particular, search for the paragraph that begins "One day Bully recounted a story".)

Psychotherapy with Children and Adolescents.

Kids are people, too, and everything I've said so far about psychotherapy applies to them as well as to adults. Still, they do need some special handling. At the most obvious level, most children do not enter psychotherapy because they want to; instead, someone around them says "This kid needs help." Resistance is therefore likely to be much higher. It may take more sessions to see progress than it would with an adult. Also, the therapist will need some extra charisma, charm, and a thicker skin than does a therapist who sees willing adults.

This is not to imply that children must be fooled. Quite the contrary. Children detect and reject phony appeals as fast, and more ruthlessly, than do adults. By the same token, however, they respond all the more eagerly to honesty and candor. Sometimes such qualities provide all a child needs to get unstuck and resume his natural development, as we saw with Mike early in this chapter.

Claire from chapter 1 is another who responded to me largely because I didn't try to be other than genuine with her. By contrast her parents, for the best of reasons, told her a lie; they said that she could do anything she wanted, which Claire then interpreted this to mean that she was crazy, disgusting, or something else awful when she could not. They ignored her often obviously substandard performances instead of helping her take some healthy perspective on them. Her teachers, for various reasons including political pressure, behaved the same way. Thus, Claire was never told that it was OK to be different, to fail at certain tasks, to have limits. (Yes, this is an example of psychological insights sounding hopelessly obvious.)

Without that validation of the reality she was perceiving, the encouragement she heard from her parents and teachers left her feeling crazy. Everyone around her acted like nothing was wrong, while she saw how far behind her peers she lagged. She felt like the child in "The Emperor's New Clothes", but without that little boy's belief in his perceptions. Somewhere just out of conscious control, the words she heard from adults were at war with her own real life experiences of failure and inadequacy; they were lies but she could not identify them as such and ignore them or take them in the spirit intended. This of course contributed greatly to her constant high tension level. So simply hearing her perceptions validated out loud by me was a tremendous relief to her.

Claire and Mike bring up another feature of psychotherapy with children. Sometimes the therapist's input feels very wrong to other adults in the child's life. How then can a parent or guardian choose a psychotherapist for a child? First, seek the credentials you want. Know that there are therapists who specialize in children. Again, go to people in your community whom you trust and who may themselves work with children; ask them who they can recommend. Then, go and meet the therapist and see if you can imagine your child warming up to him.

Once your child is involved in treatment, it will be important to keep an open mind. All the resistance I have discussed in this book may arise in you and interfere with treatment. You may find that you want to dismiss the therapist as a quack, as trying to blame parents for everything, as not on your side, and even as seducing your child away from you. Or the therapist may seem overly harsh and your natural instinct will be to rush in and save your child from this nut you foolishly thought might help.

But before yanking your child out of treatment, consider: You hire a therapist because your child is suffering (or insufferable). Even more than with adult psychotherapy the therapist accomplishes his goals by forming a relationship with your child, quite possibly the one you yourself would like to have. He becomes the child's confidant and friend, helping him become unstuck so he can resume his natural development – in short, he becomes a good parent. This is in fact the goal. It is how the child therapist makes a difference. At the same time, be assured that no matter how close that friendship, the therapist can't take your place. So keep in contact with the therapist, ask what you need to know, but accept that you may be uncomfortable with the process and even a little jealous.

Be prepared as well for a possibly bumpy ride. One of the unpleasant facts of psychotherapy with children is that a child may need help because of something going on in the family. As this material comes out in sessions, the child may become different at home, and not necessarily in pleasant ways. He may become angrier for a time, sad, argumentative, self-righteous, or otherwise difficult. If there are indeed destructive interpersonal patterns in the family, you the adult may well find yourself resenting the therapist and even the child. Hard as it may be, try to keep an open mind and to talk to the therapist about what is happening. A child is part of a family group and when one member of a group changes, all others may be unsettled. This process can be painful even when the family interactions are not particularly problematic.

One common pattern is that of the child who gave everyone in the house a person with whom to enact their needs to feel wanted, loved, needed, important. If during the course of treatment the child becomes more independent, other members of the family are now going to have unsatisfied needs; they may even feel abandoned, helpless, unappreciated. This can cause tension, dissent, unhappiness among any or all members, and it often causes resistance to the treatment.

Of course, it is not always resistance when you perceive negative things about the child's therapist. There are therapists who do side unreasonably with the children, who don't explain things to parents, or who are simply incompetent. Just as in adult psychotherapy, you should be able to understand and appreciate the reasoning behind a therapist's practices. You should see progress or understand why none is apparent. Psychotherapy is hard to put into words, so you may have to continue on faith for a while in the hope that things will become clear. But as with adult treatment, you and the therapist should agree on the time frame for this. While you don't want to pull your child out of treatment the first time you feel uncomfortable or uncertain about it, neither do you want to continue month after month with no return. (I find that the same time frame works for children and adults – 5 sessions at the most to know if we are moving in some useful direction, another 10 to see some improvement.)

Psychotherapy with Couples.

Couples work is somewhat different from individual psychotherapy. Mainly, the therapist does not climb into the individual experience of a person with the same persistence and intensity. Instead the therapist focuses more on the communication between you and your partner. He will try to bring into awareness the layers of meanings and the unspoken agendas of what goes on <u>between</u> the two of you, as opposed to what goes on inside one or the other of you. Of course, he will at times have to bring out the latter as well, but when that becomes paramount it is probably time to consider individual psychotherapy.

The goal of couples therapy is to restore communication. A relationship is only as strong as the communication between the partners. All else is secondary. When the communication fails, the relationship dies or becomes destructive; we saw examples of this in chapter 1.

The road to this goal of resuming productive communication is the same as in individual psychotherapy: Increased awareness yielding changes in feelings and behavior. And like individual psychotherapy, the work should have a logic and excitement to it; it should be more than advice, someone telling you how to manage your relationship. And if there is no improvement in 10 or 15 sessions, if you and your companion are still bickering in the same useless way, if whatever patterns you have been stuck in have not begun to change, consider a change in therapist or in the type of treatment.

I'd like to indulge in one observation from my work with couples, and it's been supported by research. As physicians have been moaning since the breed was invented: Why do you all wait so long to see me? By the time many couples come in, they have built up so many years of dissatisfaction, resentment, disgust, and eventually loathing, that it becomes a Herculean task for them just to sit in the same room together. I've had too many cases like that; the example of Carl, in chapter 1, is unfortunately not unique. Why wait until the rash has spread all over your skin and burrowed into your deeper body tissue before applying the Calamine lotion? Surely earlier treatment will prove a lot faster, easier, and cheaper. So if you and your partner have quirks, little bumps in your interactions that eat at you and don't seem to resolve in your minds and hearts, don't wait until one of you is ready to walk out! Go and sort it out with an expert in human feelings and communication – one definition of a psychotherapist.

Group Psychotherapy and Support Groups.

Resistance in group psychotherapy is notoriously higher than in individual and couples psychotherapy. Don't be surprised if more experienced group leaders require you to commit for 10 or more sessions before considering you. This is because just about everyone wants to leave the group for the first 3 months or so. You may spend about that much time being self-conscious and defensively thinking it's all garbage (unless you're right, it's defensive).

Once that resistance is broken through, group therapy can be a very powerful, eye-opening experience. It is often used as an adjunct to individual psychotherapy, rather than as the sole treatment. If you cannot afford individual psychotherapy and you want to try a group, be cautious about joining a group with a stated theme. Sometimes this can be useful in a time-limited manner, such as if you really want to focus only on the issue of the loss of your parent, spouse, or child, or if you are coping with an overwhelming and new medical problem.

Otherwise, and this is my bias, of course, given all we've discussed in this book I am suspicious of a group in which one discusses only "Men's Issues" or "Bereavement". If you've followed me this far, you know that we are all suffering in similar ways, underneath the particulars of our symptoms. All psychotherapy patients have all been bereaved in some form, even if we haven't suffered a recent real world loss; and often the bereavements we pay the least attention to are those causing the most problems. Remember that Tom thought little about his experiences with his father; he thought he was upset about creditors, his wife, his employees, and his phobias. The more you limit the range of exploration and discussion, the less you will learn about your problems and yourself.

The preceding paragraph does not apply to what are called "Support Groups". A support group is not psychotherapy, although it can be a powerful agent of change. A support group is a coming together of people with a common concern to share their experiences, feelings, and sometimes guidance. Often such groups are not led by licensed therapists but by laymen. This has been the basis of all the 12 step groups, which I believe are never led by a professional.

Support groups can be quite formidable, either as an adjunct to psychotherapy or as the sole mode of treatment. I have seen many people completely change their lives armed only with their own readiness to do so and a good 12 step program.

Medication.

Like Freud, much maligned, much misunderstood. I mentioned earlier that if you need immediate relief from seriously disruptive symptoms, sometimes medication is your only choice. This applies to intense panic attacks, other serious anxiety symptoms (hives, heart palpitations, dizziness), severe and debilitating depression, severe obsessive behavior (hand washing, counting, checking, other behavior rituals, ruminating, persistent worry), violence and other antisocial behaviors, and psychosis. Psychosis is a severe break with what most of us consider reality – the paranoid who believes Martians are living in the basement and manipulating his mind during sleep, the schizophrenic who hears voices commanding him to commit dangerous or bizarre acts, or John from my first year in graduate school (discussed early in this chapter).

Medication is also quite useful and at times necessary in many, less flamboyant situations. This is another reason for my bias that you should seek a widely experienced psychotherapist rather than someone who specializes too narrowly. The former therapist will, I believe, be best able to detect when medication should be considered.

During her first two years of treatment, Jill made tremendous changes. (This is the same woman I discussed in Chapter 5.) At first volatile, angry, intolerant of me, constantly feeling persecuted but covering it up with contempt and dismissal, she gradually relaxed. These intense negative feelings eased, she enjoyed her work more and did better at it, and she began to have more satisfying relationships.

But she still complained about "my hyperactive brain". She could not stop the endless and oppressive hypothesizing over issues large and small. Her head spun out a relentless stream of alternate possibilities, "what if"s, and "maybe"s, none of which ever really contributed to her decision-making or her happiness. We had both hoped that this obsessing would diminish as her general anxiety level went down. The emotional tone did change from harsh negativity (such as "see?! I can't decide anything! I don't know anything!") to a more neutral tone of merely reciting and endlessly reviewing the alternatives, but the obsessing itself continued. Rather reluctantly, she consulted a psychiatrist and began a low dose of medication.

The change was undeniable. She began coming into sessions with the same issues as before, but now we could work towards understanding and resolution without the constant distraction and agonizing on her part. Outside of treatment, she began to feel more relaxed, to think more clearly, to enjoy everything more, and to make decisions with much greater ease.

Will Jill be on medication forever? That depends entirely on how she feels. Many people need medication for a time, then can stop taking it with no ill effects. When will Jill stop? As with the psychotherapy, when she wants to. She will decide when she feels calm and strong enough to weather life without the aid of the medication. It is possible that she will never be able to quiet the obsessing without medication. That is unfortunate, but to my mind no more so than having to take thyroid medication throughout one's life to stabilize the metabolism, or having to take eye drops to control glaucoma. You have to remember to do it and sometimes there are side effects, but the rewards are more than worth it.

The example of Jill should show that medication is not a substitute for psychotherapy. Jill needed both treatments. The medication that helped her stop obsessing would not have stopped her lifelong habits of feeling angry, blamed, and victimized, nor changed the personality and repertoire of behavior she developed in response to these feelings. Personalities – lifelong ways of experiencing the world and one's self, whole behavioral repertoires – do not evaporate because of a pill. A pill can quiet the emotional storm, but that is often insufficient to change lifelong habits. (Research has shown this as well; the data indicate clearly that psychotherapy is at least as effective as medication, often more so.)

Important: Although it is tempting, I do not recommend going to the family physician for a prescription of psychiatric medication. Unless you luck into the right medication quickly, this route can be discouraging. Psychiatric medication requires a specialist to sift through all the vagaries and subtle differences among medicines and among patients in order to select the best one for you. Furthermore, one's inner life – one's thoughts, feelings, perceptions, experiences – are difficult to describe. You should be seeing an expert who can tease out of your words just what hurts and how a medication is affecting you. Don't skimp on money or effort in this area.

Biofeedback.

Biofeedback can be a useful adjunct to psychotherapy; on rare occasions, it is a sufficient by itself. It is useful particularly for calming anxiety and has been helpful for people who struggle with high blood pressure and other physical stress reactions. In biofeedback, a machine monitors physical functions you cannot directly see, such as heart rate, deep muscle tension, even brain waves. The readings of the instruments are converted into visual or auditory feedback which you can directly perceive, such as blips on an oscilloscope screen or beeps in a headphone. Using this feedback, you learn to control those physical functions directly. For example, if you get extremely anxious when you have to speak in public, you might use biofeedback to learn to identify how, physically, your anxiety surfaces in such situations and to quiet it so you can think straight and function.

Like most skills, biofeedback works only if you keep it up. Several of my patients have had success with it, but then laziness sets in, life's too busy, and soon the learned techniques fall by the wayside. When seeking a biofeedback center, approach it with the same active thoughtfulness with which I have encouraged you to approach a new therapist. Get answers that make sense to you, know what they are doing and why they do it. The more you are involved in the treatment program, the more likely you are to stick to it after the training is over.

Biofeedback is currently being used to treat attention deficit, under the unwieldy name of "neuro-bio-feedback". Some initial research is finding success rates comparable to those of Ritalin, the standard and quite useful treatment for attention problems in both adults and children. But remember that biofeedback requires attention and some discipline to learn the techniques, assets that may well be lacking in someone with an attention deficit.

Hypnosis.

Hypnosis is a useful adjunct to psychotherapy at times, but don't expect miracles. You rarely recover whole areas of forgotten experience, visit past lives, or quit smoking solely by using hypnosis, although hypnosis has performed well on that last task. There are only a few situations where you would want to go straight to a hypnotist. If you specifically want to explore a forgotten experience, a hypnotherapist might be able to help. Also, if you are in psychotherapy and want to see if such things as post-hypnotic suggestion (telling yourself to be calm, for example, in upcoming situations) can help, try it.

Otherwise, bear in mind that a good hypnotherapist must first be a good psychotherapist. If you are going to pursue this kind of treatment, go to someone with the credentials and qualities you want from your psychotherapist. A better plan, I believe, is to find the best psychotherapist you can. Then, and only then, discuss with the therapist the use of hypnosis in addition. And again try to get a referral directly from someone you know and trust.

Closing Thoughts.

In this book, as I do in my practice, I have been stressing as much your role in psychotherapy as my own. The single most important piece of data in a psychotherapy session is your response to it. If a therapist's interpretations and insight don't fly with you, they won't help.

Mary, age 38, came into session one day preoccupied by an article she'd read. The article described filmmaker George Lucas putting 200 million dollars of his own money into a new digital technique of filmmaking, one that would completely eliminate the need for a film set or studio. Mary is a composer; she was sad to think that she lacks that "visionary" sense, that push to newer and better and bigger. As we discussed some specific data in this regard, however, including a piece she had written for amplified violin, she began to see that she does have her own way of "pushing the envelope". On further thought, she realized that in filmmaking her push would differ from Lucas'; it would be towards greater realism in the acting, coupled with more heightened emotion, greater theatricality. In all of this she was talking too fast and said she'd been unable to get herself working the previous day because she was "antsy" after reading the article.

At this point, I was thinking that with all this rather intellectual talk she was fleeing some more central feelings of inadequacy. She suggested she was feeling a kind of "mature sorrow" (her words) in seeing one's limitations – that she was unlikely to make such a film given her career choice. I felt that an equally plausible explanation for her uncomfortable feelings, especially given the agitation I saw, was the much more common feeling of inadequacy and inferiority next to the accomplishments of others – a theme early in our work together. In short, I thought she might be lying to herself about what she was experiencing.

Which of us was right? As always, we find out by reference to data, specifically to Mary's reflections on her feelings as I inquired further. By her own description, the feeling was one of wistful sadness. As we explored what she was experiencing, it became clear that it was not the driven, panicky anxiety that usually characterizes her experiences of envy and inadequacy next to others; and she calmed down as she talked about it. It was, as she had stated, sorrow of not being able to do everything in life and not a deeper anxiety.

What I'm trying to emphasize here is that neither Mary nor I could get anywhere without her active and honest exploration of what she was feeling at the moment. In fact, without that exploration the entire discussion is rather pointless. It is only she who can tell us if we're getting anywhere useful. It is only via her effort to get to the bottom of her experience that we discover what she was feeling and thereby where she stands in her emotional development, what if anything is really bothering her and what to do about it.

Without you actively testing out the ideas that come up in sessions and seeing if they truly apply to your life, psychotherapy does not happen; no lies are uncovered, no discoveries are made that will help you feel and do better. It degenerates into a thought experiment, a series of entertaining speculations and intellectual exercises that have no impact on your life, your behavior, your feelings.

Psychotherapy is among other things a dialog, a dialectic. You present data (all the while resisting, of course), the therapist offers ideas about that data, based on his perceptions of you, his feelings and reactions, his own history. Then you pick up the ball, and so on. In the end, you must decide: Has the therapist helped you discover truth about yourself or is he up a tree? No therapist will be right all the time. There are always wrong turns and blind alleys in a session. The final word is always yours. Your therapist can tell you what <u>seems</u> to be going on with you and where you seem to be lying, from his vantage point outside your skin. Hopefully he'll be right much of the time. It is you who must decide if he is.

ACKNOWLEDGEMENTS

I'm extremely grateful to Patrick Dahdal and especially Margaret Jackins; they got me to write this. My own journey out of the lies was long. My deepest thanks go to you who gave me help above and beyond the call: Margaret Jackins, Robyn Pearl, Edgar Law, Eva Kafka Baron, Diane Quinn, Melissa Broder, Sophie Gergely, Emily Norton, Ray Arrucci, Leo Sawitz, and Gerry Perlman. I'm lucky that it all led me to the profession that has blessed my life and to the brave, hard-working patients I have been fortunate to know.

BENNETT POLOGE, PH.D.

Made in the USA
Las Vegas, NV
21 October 2020